The Active World

Landforms and Hazards

Peter Jones
and
Bob Pike

Acknowledgements

Associated Press
Barnaby's Picture Library
The Controller of Her Majesty's Stationery Office (Crown Copyright p.10)
The Countryside Commission
P. E. Baylis, University of Dundee
Peter Evans
Robert Harding
Hayward Associates
The Illustrated London News Picture Library
Isle of Wight Tourist Board
Michael Jay Publications: J. Murray Gray/J. E. Guest/Gabe Thomas
Bridget Kendall
Leeds Leisure Services
Meteorological Office Library
Mountain Equipment, Stalybridge, England
Northumbria Water
OXFAM: Jeremy Hartley/Luke Holland
Steve Reed
Usborne Publishing
Malcolm Watson

Design by Peter Smith

Illustrations by Terry Bambrook, Denby Designs, Barrie Richardson and
Ray Mutimer.

Cover photography: GeoScience Features Picture Library

The publishers have made every effort to trace all the copyright holders, but
if they have inadvertently overlooked any, they will be pleased to make the
necessary arrangements at the first opportunity.

Thomas Nelson and Sons Ltd
Nelson House Mayfield Road
Walton-on-Thames Surrey
KT12 5PL UK

51 York Place
Edinburgh
EH1 3JD UK

Thomas Nelson (Hong Kong) Ltd
Toppan Building 10/F
22A Westlands Road
Quarry Bay Hong Kong

Thomas Nelson Australia
102 Dodds Street
South Melbourne
Victoria 3205 Australia

Nelson Canada
1120 Birchmount Road
Scarborough Ontario
MIK 5G4 Canada

© 1986 Peter Jones and Bob Pike

First published by Arnold-Wheaton (a division of E J Arnold and Son Ltd) 1986
(under ISBN 0-560-26520-4)

First published by Thomas Nelson and Sons Ltd 1991

ISBN 0-17-434266-7
NPN 9 8 7 6 5 4 3 2

Printed in Great Britain

Contents

Active Earth

The world we live on is a very complicated but very delicate arrangement of **scenery** and living things. There are an increasing number of signs that this delicate arrangement is being upset. The balance of nature is being disturbed by human activity. The photographs show some examples:

- **equatorial forests** are being cut down very rapidly, an area the size of the United Kingdom is destroyed each year
- in the Sahel region of northern Africa, overgrazing around waterholes is turning the tropical **savanna grasslands** into **desert**
- mining, quarrying and the dumping of waste provides necessary products and services but also destroys the natural scenery

fig 1

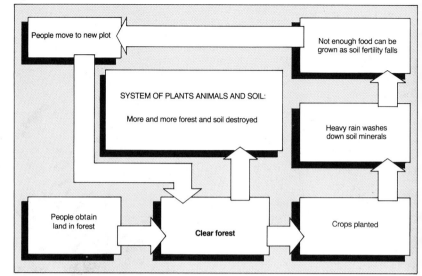

fig 2

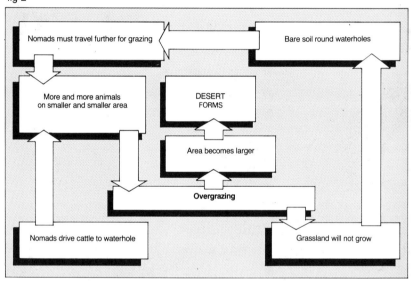

fig 3

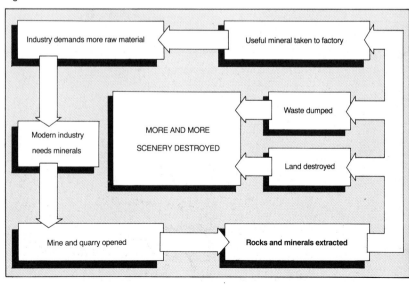

Out of Balance

photo 1: Clearing of forest

photo 2: Drought in the Sahel

photo 3: Mining Waste

There have been many more environmental problems caused by humans in the last 200 years than in the whole of previous history. The three shown here are only a few of many. The diagrams show how these problems are caused.

Two dramatic changes have occurred in the last 200 years. Firstly there has been a massive increase in the world's population. This means we must produce extra food and resources. Secondly the development of industrial technology has meant that we are using more fuel and other natural resources than ever before.

By using up resources so rapidly we are putting the earth's natural system out of balance. This could easily ruin the world for people both now and in the future.

Activity B

These questions can be done in groups or individually.

1 Choose one of the problems in the diagrams.

a in your notebook copy the diagram of the problem.

b describe in sentences the photograph illustrating your problem.

c in your own words write down how the problem arose.

2 Try to write a list of problems. Write as many as you can think of, similar to the ones on this page (such as acid rain and polluted rivers). Then study the diagrams shown, and illustrate one of the problems on your list in the same way. Do this on a large sheet of paper, to act as a wall chart.

A Simple System

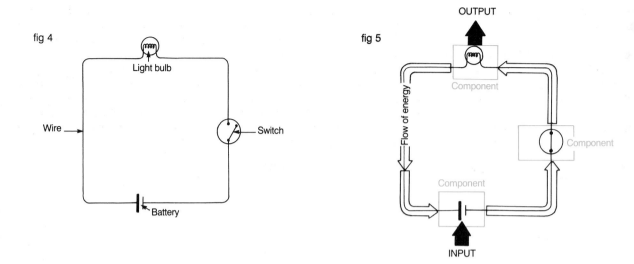

fig 4

Light bulb

Wire

Switch

Battery

fig 5

OUTPUT

Component

Flow of energy

Component

Component

INPUT

Fig 4 is an example of a simple system. It shows that a system has three different features:
- **component parts** battery, wires, switch and lamp
- **flows of energy** linking the parts such as an **input** of electricity from the battery
- **outputs** resulting from the parts working together such as light

If any part of the system is changed or damaged, then the whole system is affected. The flow of energy is altered and the output becomes different. The whole system gets out of balance or does not work.

Photo 4 shows a simple electrical circuit. You can see a light connected by wires to a battery. There is a switch in the circuit. When the switch is in the on position the parts or **components** are all connected together, and the current can flow from the battery through the wire and the lamp lights up. This is a simple **system** where all the parts work together to give light, a result which each part on its own cannot give. We can show this system in a diagram like fig 5.

The light works because all the components are in balance. If the current provided by the battery is too strong for the light bulb the balance is upset. The light bulb will burn out or blow. The system therefore breaks down.

photo 4

Activity A
1 Continue making your dictionary of geography by describing each of the words in bold type.
2 When you are riding a bicycle you become part of a working system. You provide the input or energy, the parts of the bicycle work together and the result is that you move forward. If your chain comes off the system breaks down. Draw two diagrams, similar to those on this page, which show
a the you-bicycle system working
b the you-bicycle system breaking down
Can you think of other ways this system can break down? List them.
3 Now try to list examples of other simple systems which have components, energy flows and outputs.

System Earth

The earth is a very large system. Like all systems it has:

- many component parts, such as **continents,** oceans, **atmosphere**, rocks, and scenery
- energy, which mainly comes from the sun
- outputs, which can be thought of as the life which it supports

However, it is extremely complicated because it is made up of millions of smaller and smaller systems.

These earth systems, just like the electrical circuit, are all naturally in balance. When they are disturbed or overloaded then they get out of balance, and all parts of the system do not work together. The effect or output is changed in some way and

this may lead to the kind of problems of **environmental** damage or disaster shown in the three problems on pages 4 and 5.

Since these problems affect people's lives, it is important to know how the earth's systems work and how people can either prevent them getting out of balance, or try to put them back in balance.

fig 6   THERE ARE FIVE MAIN SYSTEMS WHICH ALL WORK TOGETHER

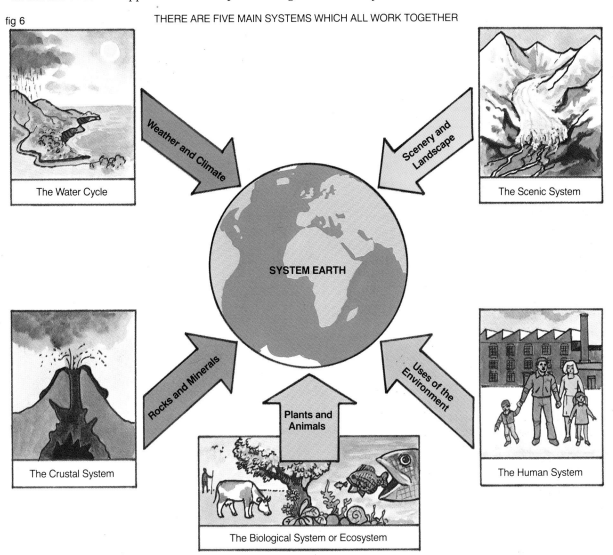

The Water Cycle

The Scenic System

SYSTEM EARTH

Weather and Climate

Scenery and Landscape

Rocks and Minerals

Uses of the Environment

Plants and Animals

The Crustal System

The Human System

The Biological System or Ecosystem

The subject of **geography** studies the natural and human systems which make up the earth and how it works. Since it is so complicated, we study it by looking at each system individually. This book looks at a number of natural systems and how they affect the way in which people live. The first of these is the system of weather.

Activity B
Look at fig 6.
Name the five main systems which make up **system earth**. The arrows show the output of each of these five systems. Use the diagram to help you complete the table.

SYSTEM	OUTPUT
	Weather and Climate
Scenic	
	Rocks and minerals
	Plants and animals
Human	

Weather and People

We are all affected by the **weather** in many ways. Did you wear a coat to school this morning? Was the weather good on your holiday? What is the weather like outside? We all experience weather, from being soaked by rain to sweltering in a heat wave.

For some people the weather is vitally important to their work, and in some cases even lives can be in danger. The cartoons show some examples:

fig 7

Storm at sea (1)

Sheep in snow (2)

Traffic and fog (3)

Holidays (6)

Hurricane fury (4)

Harvest home (5)

Activity A

1 For each picture write one sentence describing the effect of the weather. For example: 'Picture (1) shows how a storm at sea can upset fishing vessels and require lifeboat crews to risk their lives in rescue'.
2 Try to list at least five other jobs where the work is affected by the weather.
3 Draw a cartoon to show one of them, and write a sentence similar to the ones you wrote describing our pictures to describe your own.
4 There are many words which deal with weather, such as rain, thermometer, dull, visibility, wet, dry. How many can you write down? One pupil recently found 258. Can you beat that total?

'Rain before seven, fine before eleven'
'Red sky at night, shepherd's delight
Red sky in morning, shepherd's warning'
There are many such proverbs and sayings about the weather. Use the school and public libraries to find as many as you can.

Features of Weather

The three photographs show some of the features of weather. All weather features can be measured. These measurements are written down and studied. The study of these records is known as **meteorology**. The records are collected at the Central Meteorological Office and are turned into weather maps or charts. The features of weather which are normally measured are:

- **temperature** in degrees Celsius
- **humidity** dampness of the air
- **cloudiness** type and amount of cloud
- **condensation** dew, frost, mist and fog
- **precipitation** rain, drizzle, sleet, snow and hail
- **sunshine** number of hours of sunshine each day
- **air pressure** weight of air pressing down
- **wind** speed and direction
- **visibility** distance that it is possible to see
- **thunder and lightning**

These features are the outputs of the world **weather system**

Activity B

Answer each question with a sentence.

1 Which components of the weather are shown in the photos?
2 What are the other components of weather?
3 What is meteorology? Add this definition to your dictionary of geography.
4 What is the technical word for each of the following:
a weight of air.
b distance you can see.
c how damp the air is.
d drizzle, rain, sleet, snow and hail.
5 Add to your dictionary of geography definitions for all the components of weather.
6 What is the output of the weather system?

photo 5

photo 6

photo 7

Recording the Weather

Recording the features of weather needs accurate observation of each feature. This is done at **weather recording stations**. These stations contain a number of instruments such as:

- **thermometer** which measures temperature
- **hygrometer** a wet and dry bulb thermometer to measure humidity
- **rain gauge** which measures precipitation
- **sunshine recorder** to record hours of sunshine
- **barometer** for measuring air pressure
- **anemometer** to measure wind speed
- **wind vane** to show the wind direction

Other weather components are observed and recorded directly:

- types of clouds
- amount of cloud:
  how many eighths of the sky is covered by cloud, this is written down as **oktas**
- visibility
- special weather events such as thunder, lightning, dew, fog, frost and mist

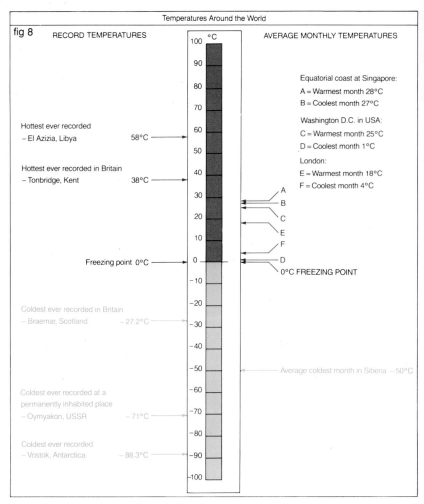

Temperatures Around the World

fig 8 RECORD TEMPERATURES

AVERAGE MONTHLY TEMPERATURES

°C

Equatorial coast at Singapore:
A = Warmest month 28°C
B = Coolest month 27°C

Washington D.C. in USA:
C = Warmest month 25°C
D = Coolest month 1°C

London:
E = Warmest month 18°C
F = Coolest month 4°C

Hottest ever recorded
– El Azizia, Libya   58°C

Hottest ever recorded in Britain
– Tonbridge, Kent   38°C

0°C FREEZING POINT

Freezing point 0°C

Coldest ever recorded in Britain
– Braemar, Scotland   – 27.2°C

Average coldest month in Siberia – 50°C

Coldest ever recorded at a
permanently inhabited place
– Oymyakon, USSR   – 71°C

Coldest ever recorded
– Vostok, Antarctica   – 88.3°C

photo 8: A Stevenson screen

We all have different ideas of what is hot or cold. To obtain an unbiased view measurements are usually taken from thermometers hung in the shade where air can circulate round them, in a box called a **Stevenson screen.**

Separate thermometers are used to record the highest (maximum) and lowest (minimum) temperatures.

Activity A

1 Use fig 8
a what temperature is the highest recorded?
b what temperature is the lowest recorded?
2 Why are thermometers kept in a Stevenson screen?
3 Draw a labelled diagram of a Stevenson screen.

Clouds

Humidity is the dampness of the air, or the amount of **water vapour** it contains. When air rises, it cools. When cooled enough, the water vapour condenses into millions of tiny water droplets. These come together to form clouds.

Although no two clouds are exactly alike they can be grouped into three types, depending on their shape and height:

- **cirrus** very high cloud made of ice crystals
- **cumulus** a cloud in the shape of a heap
- **stratus** a cloud in the shape of a layer

These types can be sub-divided as the cloud diagram shows.

If the droplets of water or ice in clouds grow so heavy that the air cannot support them, they fall to the ground as rain, hail, snow or sleet. We call this **precipitation**. Clouds giving precipitation have the word **nimbus** added to their name.

When clouds form at ground level they give mist and fog.

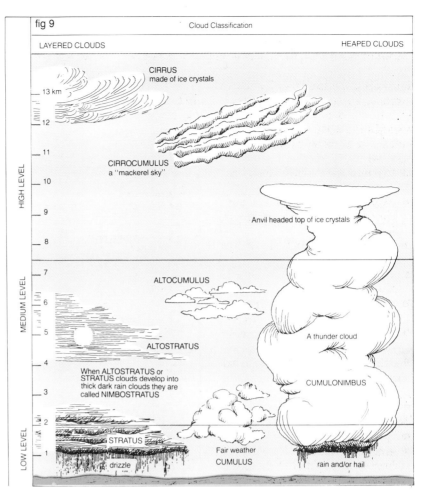

fig 9 — Cloud Classification

LAYERED CLOUDS — HEAPED CLOUDS

HIGH LEVEL
- CIRRUS made of ice crystals — 13 km
- CIRROCUMULUS a "mackerel sky"
- Anvil headed top of ice crystals

MEDIUM LEVEL
- ALTOCUMULUS
- ALTOSTRATUS
- When ALTOSTRATUS or STRATUS clouds develop into thick dark rain clouds they are called NIMBOSTRATUS
- A thunder cloud
- CUMULONIMBUS

LOW LEVEL
- STRATUS
- drizzle
- Fair weather CUMULUS
- rain and/or hail

photo 9: A snowflake micrograph

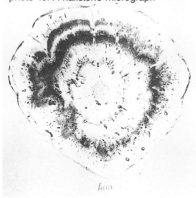

photo 10: A hailstone micrograph

Activity B

1 Add a definition of each of the words in bold type, and the cloud names to your dictionary of geography.

2 Write down how snow, hailstones and rain are formed.

3 Keep a Cloud Diary for a fortnight. Record twice a day the following things:

a the type of cloud
b the wind direction
c the weather

Look out for any links between wind, clouds and weather. Does one type of cloud usually have the same wind and weather? Draw a cloud diagram like the one above to show the clouds you recorded.

A lot of people think that snow is frozen rain, but this is not true. Snow forms when water vapour condenses very quickly straight into ice crystals (see photo 9).

Hailstones begin as raindrops. If a small raindrop is carried by an upward air current high into a cumulus cloud it will freeze. Each time this happens an extra layer of ice is added making the hailstone bigger and bigger. When cut in half the layers forming the hailstone can be clearly seen (see photo 10).

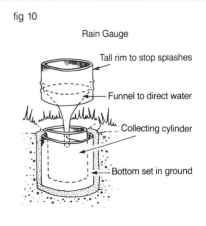

fig 10

Rain Gauge
- Tall rim to stop splashes
- Funnel to direct water
- Collecting cylinder
- Bottom set in ground

Windy Days

Weather forecasters want to know two things about the wind: speed and direction.

An **anemometer** measures wind speed. Its direction (the compass bearing from which it came) is shown by a **wind vane**.

fig 11

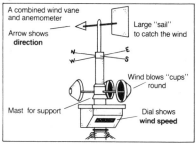

A combined wind vane and anemometer
Arrow shows **direction**
Large "sail" to catch the wind
Wind blows "cups" round
Mast for support
Dial shows **wind speed**

In 1805, Admiral Sir Francis Beaufort worked out a guide to the amount of sail that a ship of the Royal Navy could safely spread at different speeds of the wind. His scale went from calm (force 0) to hurricane (force 12).

A version of the scale showing the effects that winds of different speeds have over land is shown in the table.

fig 12 **BEAUFORT'S SCALE OF WIND**			
SCALE FORCE	WIND NAME	SPEED in km/hr	WIND EFFECTS ON LAND
0	CALM AIR	0 – 1	Calm; smoke rises vertically
1	LIGHT AIR	1 – 3	Direction of wind shown by smoke, but not by wind vanes
2	LIGHT BREEZE	4 – 11	Wind felt on face; leaves rustle; ordinary vane moved by wind
3	GENTLE BREEZE	12 – 19	Leaves and small twigs constantly moving; wind extends small flag
4	MODERATE BREEZE	20 – 29	Raises dust and loose paper; small branches are moved
5	FRESH BREEZE	30 – 39	Small trees in leaf begin to sway; little wave crests form on inland waters
6	STRONG BREEZE	40 – 50	Large branches move; whistling heard in telephone wires; umbrellas used with difficulty
7	MODERATE GALE	51 – 61	Whole trees move; inconvenience felt when walking against the wind
8	FRESH GALE	62 – 74	Breaks twigs off trees; progress generally hindered or impeded
9	STRONG GALE	75 – 86	Slight structural damage occurs, such as roof slates or chimney pots removed
10	WHOLE GALE	87 – 101	Considerable structural damage; trees uprooted; seldom experienced inland
11	STORM	102 – 115	Very rarely experienced; accompanied by widespread damage
12	HURRICANE	OVER 115	Countryside devasted

A Pressing Matter

Each square metre of the earth's surface has about 10,000 kilogrammes of air above it. The weight of all this air on a certain area exerts a force (**air pressure**) which is measured with a **barometer**.

fig 13

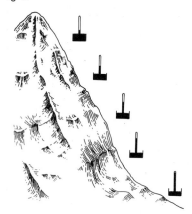

At sea level air pressure is strong enough to hold up a column of mercury some 76 cm high. The higher up a mountain you go the less air there is above you so the air pressure (and the height of the column of mercury) is less.

Mercury barometers actually have a tall tube of mercury, but the common barometer in most homes is an **aneroid barometer** which shows the air pressure on a dial. **Barographs** use a pen to make a record of the pressure on a piece of paper.

The pressure of air varies over the earth's surface and is constantly changing. Air moves from high pressure to low pressure areas. This movement of air we call wind. We need to know about pressure to forecast winds.

Activity

1 Explain what these words mean: aneroid barometer, mercury barometer, air pressure, isobar, anemometer, wind, Beaufort scale of wind speeds. Check the definitions in your dictionary.

2 Draw pictures to illustrate winds force 1, 3, 7 and 10. (Look back to page 8 where there is a drawing of a hurricane force 12.)

3 Answer these questions in sentences in your notebook.
a what is the speed of the wind when smoke rises vertically?
b what force of wind can uproot trees?
c how fast is a fresh breeze?
d what effects does a force 6 wind have?
e what force are winds that blow at 10, 20, 30, 40 and 80 km/hour?
4 What is the link between wind and pressure?

Your own Weather Station

fig 14

Date	Time	Air pressure mb	TEMPERATURE		Dampness %	WIND		Cloud amount Oktas	Precipitation mm	Visibility	Name: Billy Jenkins
			Minimum °C	Maximum °C		Direction	Speed Knots				Any other comments Gateshead
1	9.05	1008	10	16	94	NW	10	7	9	F	Cloudy and wet
2	8.30	1010	8	17	74	NE	16	4	1	G	
3	10.00	1000	9	16	88	NW	15	6	3	F	Clouds building up
4	9.00	997	6	13	100	NW	5	8	21	F	Raining very heavily
5											
6											
7											

WEATHER DIARY   Month: June   Year: 1984

Running your own weather station is one way of studying and recording the weather. Keep a weather diary similar to the one shown above. You will have to keep it up for a long time if it is to be really worthwhile. Start keeping your diary now for the next month.

Before you begin you will need certain weather recording instruments such as:

- a rain gauge
- a thermometer
- a barometer for measuring air pressure
- an anemometer or wind sock for measuring wind speed and direction
- a hygrometer such as a wet and dry bulb thermometer for measuring humidity

You may be able to use the school weather station. The best way is to make your own versions of some of the instruments so that you can run a weather station at home.

fig 15

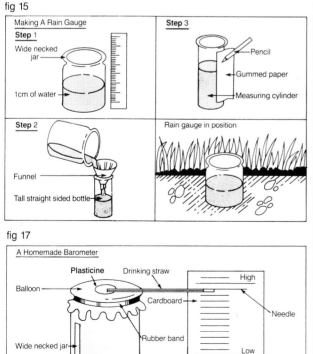

fig 16

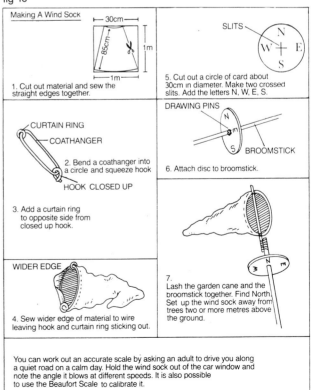

You can work out an accurate scale by asking an adult to drive you along a quiet road on a calm day. Hold the wind sock out of the car window and note the angle it blows at different speeds. It is also possible to use the Beaufort Scale to calibrate it.

Changing Weather

The next few pages show the weather during the third week of April 1983. The records shown are:

- a page from a pupil's weather diary recording the components of weather you have just studied
- a weather satellite photograph of the type you often see on TV
- a TV style weather summary chart
- a weather summary chart

These are four different ways of showing the same thing.

Activity A

Study the four diagrams showing the weather of day one (13 April 1983).

1 What was the highest recorded temperature on this day at Newcastle upon Tyne?
2 What was the wind speed at the time of observation?
3 Write 2 or 3 sentences which describe fully all the components of the weather on this day.
4 Where in Great Britain does the satellite photograph show areas of heavy cloud?
5 Look at the weather map (fig 18). On an outline map, make a copy. Add a key to your map to show what you think the symbols mean.

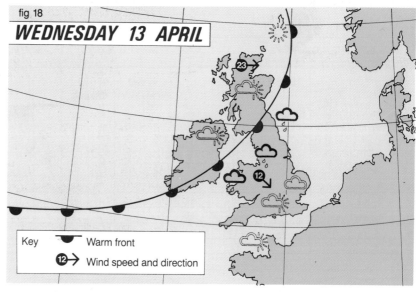

fig 18
WEDNESDAY 13 APRIL

Key — Warm front
12→ Wind speed and direction

photo 11 Satellite (13/4/83)

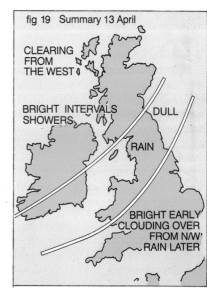

fig 19 Summary 13 April

CLEARING FROM THE WEST

BRIGHT INTERVALS SHOWERS — DULL

RAIN

BRIGHT EARLY CLOUDING OVER FROM N/W RAIN LATER

Date	Time	Air pressure m.b.	Minimum °C	Maximum °C	Dampness %	Direction	Speed Knots	Cloud amount Oktas	Precipitation m.m.	Visibility	Any other comments
fig 20	WEATHER DIARY		TEMPERATURE			WIND					Month: April Year: 1983
											Name: Jill Burgess
											Newcastle upon Tyne
1	9.00	1007	1	8	91	NE	5	7	3	F	
2	8.50	1012	0	7	79	NW	5	0	0	G	Cold bright morning
3	9.05	1006	1	6	96	NW	10	8	5	F	Just started to
12	8.55	1025	5	9	82	N	48	4	0	G	Blustery
13	9.00	1023	5	11	78	NW	12	6	0	F	

'The North Wind doth blow, And we shall have snow.'

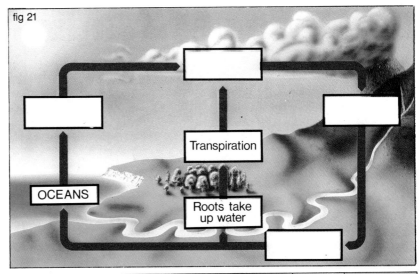

fig 21

OCEANS

Transpiration

Roots take up water

The person who first made up this famous saying, realised that the kind of weather we get in Britain depends on the direction from which the wind blows. Here are two examples:

● wind from the north in winter comes from the Arctic Ocean. It is therefore very cold and damp. It often brings winter snow to the north

● wind from the south-west comes from the tropical parts of the north Atlantic Ocean and is therefore warm and damp

Other examples are shown on the map.

A wind that has its own special temperatures and dampness in this way is called an **airstream**. The weather is changed when one airstream takes the place of another. Where two airstreams meet, the warmer one will be lighter and forced to rise. The name for the area where airstreams meet is a **front**.

When air rises it changes . We have seen what happens on page 11. Let us remind ourselves. As air rises, it becomes cooler. Since this air contains water vapour which is also rising and cooling, the water vapour will condense into millions of tiny droplets of water and ice when it is cooled enough . These form clouds. If the condensation continues, the droplets become too heavy to be held up. They fall as rain, hail, snow or sleet. We call this precipitation. The **water cycle** diagram shows all the stages by which this happens.

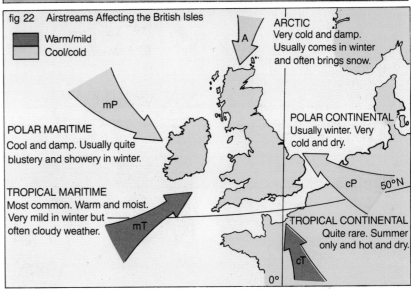

fig 22   Airstreams Affecting the British Isles

Warm/mild
Cool/cold

ARCTIC
Very cold and damp. Usually comes in winter and often brings snow.

mP

POLAR MARITIME
Cool and damp. Usually quite blustery and showery in winter.

POLAR CONTINENTAL
Usually winter. Very cold and dry.

cP   50°N

TROPICAL MARITIME
Most common. Warm and moist. Very mild in winter but often cloudy weather.

mT

TROPICAL CONTINENTAL
Quite rare. Summer only and hot and dry.

cT

0°

Activity B

1 Study the writing on this page. Work out a definition of each of the following words: airstream, front, evaporation, precipitation, run off, water cycle.
Add any new words from this list to your dictionary.
2 Draw a careful copy of the water cycle diagram (fig 21). Complete it by printing the following words in the correct boxes: evaporation, condensation, precipitation and run off.
3 Study the map of airstreams (fig 22) and the writing about them. Use them to try and complete this table in your notebook:

Name of Airstream	Wind Direction	Conditions (use words like warm, cold, damp, dry)
Arctic	N	Very cold and damp
Polar Maritime	W to NW	
Tropical Maritime		
Polar Continental		
		Very hot and dry

Patterns of Cloudiness

On day one, much of Britain was covered by an airstream from the north-west. In Scotland, a different airstream blew from the west. These airstreams met at a front, shown on the satellite picture on page 14 as a belt of heavy cloud.

On day two (April 14th) the westerly airstream moved across Great Britain in a south-easterly direction and the whole country became covered by it. Its direction began to change late in the day from a westerly to a south-westerly wind. This would mean that it should become a little warmer on day three.

fig 23

Date	Time	Air pressure m.b.	TEMPERATURE Minimum °C	TEMPERATURE Maximum °C	Dampness %	WIND Direction	WIND Speed Knots	Cloud amount Oktas	Precipitation m.m.	Visibility	Name: Jill Burgess / Any other comments
											Newcastle upon Tyne
1	9.00	1007	1	8	91	NE	5	7	3	F	
2	8.50	1012	0	7	79	NW	5	0	0	G	Cold bright morning
3	9.05	1006	1	6	96	NW	10	8	5	F	Just started to
12	8.55	1025	5	9	82	N	48	4	0	G	Blustery
13	9.00	1023	5	11	78	NW	12	6	0	F	
14	8.50	1024	6	10	88	W	18	8	4	P	Damp and overcast
15											

WEATHER DIARY Month: April Year: 1983

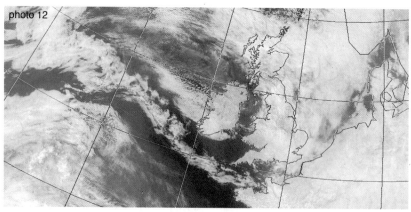

photo 12

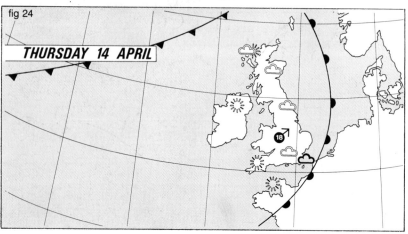

fig 24 — THURSDAY 14 APRIL

Activity A

Study the weather diagrams for day two (14th April 1983).

1 As the westerly air advanced across Great Britain it brought a little rain at its front. How much rain did it bring to Newcastle upon Tyne?

2 What type of cloud was connected with this light rain? Can you remember what shape this type of cloud has?

3 Describe all the other changes in the weather between these two days. Use the headings of the weather diary to make sure you do not forget anything.

4 Draw a summary chart for the weather of 14th April 1983, similar to the type of summary chart (fig 19) on page 14.

The satellite photographs and maps show a gradual change in the weather over the three day period. The original airstream came from the north-west but was gradually pushed away to the south-east by the westerly airstream. By the third day this airstream had gradually shifted round until it came from the south-west. It became warmer as it slightly changed its position.

The satellite photograph for day three (15th April 1983), shows another front coming towards Great Britain from the north-west. It also crossed the country by moving south-eastwards. Like all fronts it is the leading edge of a new airstream, in our case the third. It is a cool, moist airstream and will therefore bring its own weather for the following days of April 16th and 17th.

Such changes in airstreams (with moving fronts, moving bands of cloud and sometimes rain), help to explain why this weather changed so frequently.

fig 25

Date	Time	Air pressure m.b.	TEMPERATURE		Dampness %	WIND		Cloud amount Oktas	Precipitation m.m.	Visibility	Name: Jill Burgess
			Minimum °C	Maximum °C		Direction	Speed Knots				Any other comments
											Newcastle upon Tyne
1	9.00	1007	1	8	91	NE	5	7	3	F	
2	8.50	1012	0	7	79	NW	5	0	0	G	Cold bright morning
3	9.05	1006	1	6	96	NW	10	8	5	F	Just started to
12	8.55	1025	5	9	82	N	48	4	0	G	Blustery
13	9.00	1023	5	11	78	NW	12	6	0	F	
14	8.50	1024	6	10	88	W	8	8	4	P	Damp and overcast
15	8.50	1024	5	13	83	SW	3	3	0	F	Feels warmer than yesterday.

WEATHER DIARY   Month: April   Year: 1983

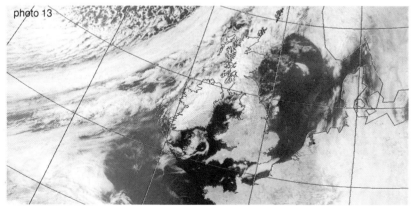

photo 13

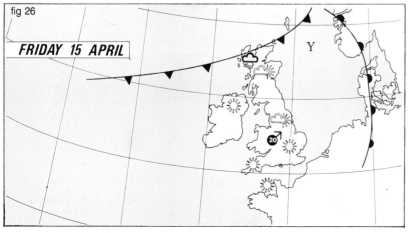

fig 26

FRIDAY 15 APRIL

Y

20

Activity B

1 Prepare another TV style summary chart for this day's weather. Notice from the TV weather map that another front is coming towards Great Britain from the north Atlantic Ocean.

2 Imagine that you are on an oil rig in the North Sea, at the point marked 'Y' on the weather map. Write a forecast for the next three days as the new front and cool, moist airstream comes south-east.

3 Keep a record of your weather over the next three days. Video record the weather forecasts and see how accurate they are.

4 See if you can write about the pattern or sequence of weather you record.

Displaying the Patterns

The three day period we have been studying is shown by the satellite photos 11 to 13. They are followed by photographs of the next three days (photos 14 to 16). These show a front with a belt of cloud and rain passing through Britain. On the 18th Britain had a new cool, moist airstream because the front had completely moved away.

Fig 27 is a weather diary for the whole of the month of April 1983 at Newcastle upon Tyne. This is one way of recording weather information. The data can be illustrated in a number of ways, the graphs on page 19 show three of them.

- rainfall only happens from time to time, for this a **bar chart** is used
- a **line graph** is used for maximum temperature, because temperature is constantly changing
- the **wind rose** shows how often the wind blows from each direction

Activity A
Refer to your table of airstreams in Activity B on page 15. Name the three airstreams affecting Britain during the six days of April 13th to 18th 1983. Use the correct technical names for each one.

fig 27

Date	Time	Air pressure m.b.	TEMPERATURE Minimum °C	TEMPERATURE Maximum °C	Dampness %	WIND Direction	WIND Speed Knots	Cloud amount Oktas	Precipitation m.m.	Visibility	Name: Jill Burgess / Any other comments / Newcastle upon Tyne
1	9.00	1007	1	8	91	NE	5	7	3	F	
2	8.50	1012	0	7	79	NW	5	0	0	G	Cold bright morning
3	9.05	1006	1	6	96	NW	10	8	5	F	Just started to rain
4	9.00	993	2	8	90	W	5	4	2	F	
5	9.30	992	0	8	78	SE	5	0	1	G	
6	8.55	990	-2	9	90	CALM		8	0	F	Frosty last night
7	8.45	995	-1	10	89	NW	3	0	0	G	Frost
8	8.50	996	2	8	96	CALM		8	1	P	
9	8.50	1007	1	11	95	NW	5	1	0	G	
10	8.55	1009	3	6	94	NE	5	8	7	F	
11	9.10	1009	1	7	97	NE	35	8	1	F	Strong winds.
12	8.55	1025	5	9	82	N	48	4	0	G	Blustery
13	9.00	1023	5	11	78	NW	12	6	0	F	
14	8.50	1024	6	10	88	W	18	8	4	P	Damp and overcast
15	8.50	1024	5	13	83	SW	23	3	0	F	Feels warmer than yesterday
16	9.00	1012	4	13	89	SW	11	8	0	F	
17	8.30	997	-1	10	82	NW	10	4	6	F	Chilly, now drizzling
18	9.00	1003	3	6	88	N	4	8	16	F	
19	9.00	1001	2	6	100	N	25	8	8	P	
20	9.05	1007	1	10	94	SW	5	4	25	P	Rained a lot in the night
21	9.05	997	1	9	100	W	24	8	1	P	Drizzling now
22	8.55	1008	5	7	97	E	5	8	6	P	
23	9.15	998	5	13	97	SW	5	8	1	F	
24	9.00	1003	4	14	83	SW	5	7	0	F	Just a trace of rain
25	8.50	1007	6	9	83	E	24	6	3	G	
26	8.55	1010	4	7	100	E	5	8	0	F	Very damp and overcast
27	9.05	1011	5	7	100	NE	3	8	15	F	
28	8.55	1008	6	7	97	NW	18	8	19	P	
29	9.10	1011	6	8	97	NW	12	8	1	P	
30	9.00	1010	5	9	91	CALM		7	0	F	

WEATHER DIARY — Month: April — Year: 1983

If you cannot find out or measure the exact figures, you could use letters or words. For example:
VISIBILITY could be G = GOOD, F = FAIR, P = POOR

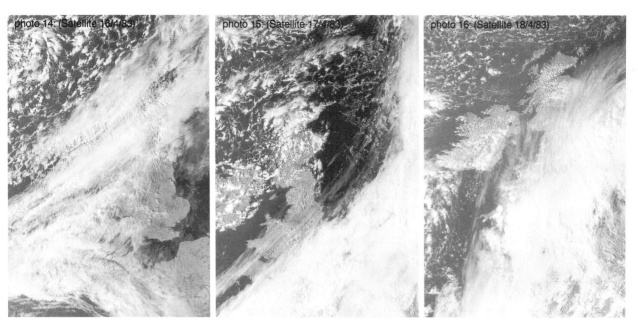

photo 14: (Satellite 16/4/83) photo 15: (Satellite 17/4/83) photo 16: (Satellite 18/4/83)

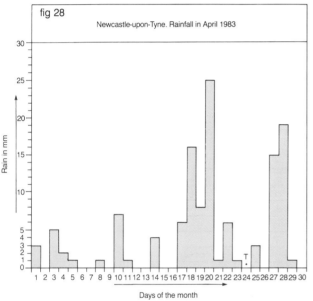

fig 28
Newcastle-upon-Tyne. Rainfall in April 1983
Rain in mm
Days of the month

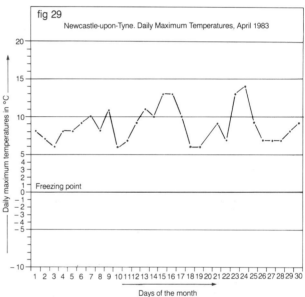

fig 29
Newcastle-upon-Tyne. Daily Maximum Temperatures, April 1983
Daily maximum temperatures in °C
Freezing point
Days of the month

fig 30

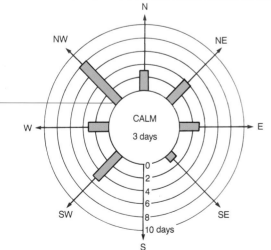

Newcastle-upon-Tyne. Recorded Daily Wind Directions, April 1983

Activity B

1 Draw an exact copy of the graph of maximum temperatures. Using the weather diary, plot the minimum temperatures for each day and draw in the line for the month, on the same graph.

2 Which day shows the greatest difference between maximum and minimum temperatures? This difference is known as the daily or **diurnal range of temperature**.

3 Draw two graphs. One to show air pressure throughout the month, and another to show cloud amount. Use two different methods for each graph.

4 Keep a weather diary, either on your own or as part of a group. Try to maintain it for one month. When you have completed your own month's record, display it on a large sheet of paper.

Forecasting Weather

The weather is important to many people in all sorts of ways because it affects their jobs and lives. It is essential that we can tell in advance or predict what the weather is going to be. This is known as **forecasting**. To be able to forecast accurately a lot of detailed and precise information is needed. This is collected by the **meteorological office** through observations from satellites, aeroplanes and ships, weather balloons and from a network of weather recording stations. Hourly around Britain, scientists record the weather details. The information is sent to the Central Meteorological Office at Bracknell in Berkshire. They also receive similar information from weather stations throughout the world.

With the help of a computer and past records the meteorological office is able to produce a chart and forecast the weather. This forecast is continually updated as more information is sent in and is what is seen or heard on television or radio and in the newspapers.

People sometimes say that the weather reports are misleading. This is not true. Most forecasts are right, nine times out of ten.

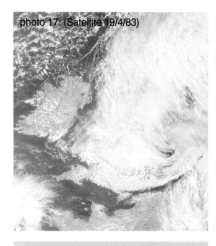
photo 17: (Satellite 19/4/83)

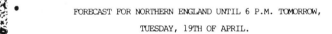

```
•        FORECAST FOR NORTHERN ENGLAND UNTIL 6 P.M. TOMORROW,      •
                    TUESDAY, 19TH OF APRIL.


  A cold north easterly airstream will cover the British Isles.  In
  northern England it will be cloudy with outbreaks of rain and snow in
  places on the hills.  Brighter and showery later, as drier weather
  spreads north in the afternoon.  Temperatures will fall to 3°C tonight
  rising to 7 or 8°C tomorrow.  Winds fresh to strong, perhaps gale force
  in places, from the north east, turning north west later.  Outlook: sunny
  periods and showers.
```

fig 31

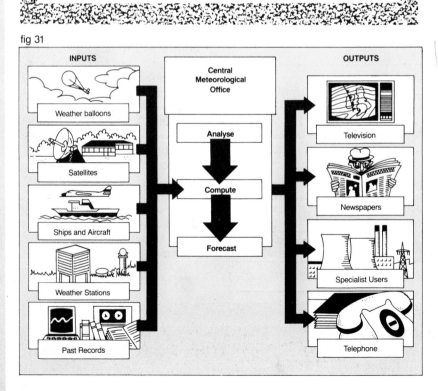

Activity A

1 Read the forecast for Tuesday, 19th April. Check it with the weather diary for the same day in Newcastle upon Tyne, fig 27, on page 18. What are the differences between the forecast and the actual weather?

2 Copy out this paragraph and fill in the gaps:
The Central Meteorological Office at . . . ., gathers in information from all over the world. Among the sources of this . . . . are . . . . orbiting the earth, ..., ships and planes and above all the . . . . With the help of the . . . . the Meteorological Office . . . . the results, compares what is happening to what has happened in the past and prepares . . . . There are many customers for these. . . . . and radio, ... and the British Telecom recorded weather service all give the details. People with special needs can pay for . . . .

Missing words: data, computer, forecasts, satellites, Bracknell, weather balloons, analyses, television, weather recording stations, newspapers, specialist forecasts.

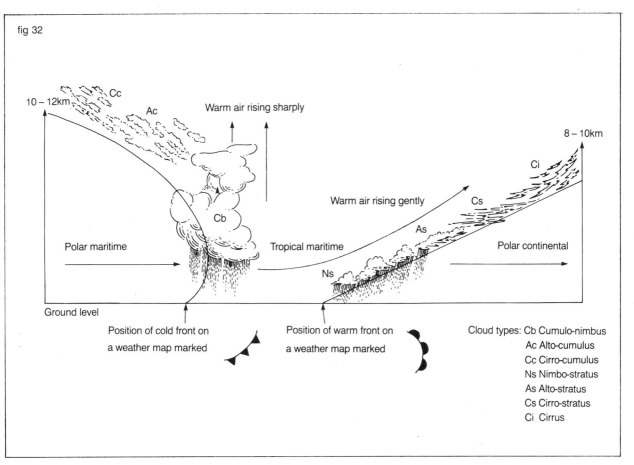

fig 32

Cloud types: Cb Cumulo-nimbus
Ac Alto-cumulus
Cc Cirro-cumulus
Ns Nimbo-stratus
As Alto-stratus
Cs Cirro-stratus
Ci Cirrus

The weather of our six-day period was affected by three different **airstreams**.

The table shows that on April 13th there was a north-westerly airstream over Britain. This was replaced on April 14th by a westerly airstream bringing different weather. It remained until April 16th when the airstream changed to a north-westerly and northerly one. The weather brought by each of these three airstreams was different. The table also shows that between each airstream a front passed, on these occasions it became cloudy or completely overcast and there was snow, sleet or rain.

Fronts are a common feature of our weather. They occur when two types of airstream meet and are usually marked on weather maps by the symbols shown in fig 32. One of the airstreams has warmer, lighter air, this causes it to rise over the other one. When air rises clouds form and precipitation may result.

Fronts normally come when the pressure of the air is **low**. Low pressure encourages the air to rise this can form clouds. Where there is low pressure it is called a **depression**. When the weather is changing a great deal it is normally associated with fronts and depressions. This occurred during our six-day period. When air pressure is **high** the air cannot usually rise. The weather is often dry and sunny. An area of high pressure is called an **anticyclone** and brings the warmest summer days.

Date	Air Stream		Weather
Wednesday 13th April	1	North westerly	Mild, cloudy, no rain.
Thursday 14th April	1 later 2	Westerly, changing to south westerly	Similar to that of 13th at first but airstream changes when a front passes. Weather is then overcast with a slight rise in temperature and a little rain.
Friday 15th April	2	South westerly	Sunny intervals with some cloud. Warm.
Saturday 16th April	2 later 3	South westerly to north westerly	Similar to Friday at first, but as airstream changes when a front passes, cloudy with some rain. Getting colder.
Sunday 17th April	3	north westerly	Below freezing at night. Some snow or sleet flurries. Cold.
Monday 18th April	3	north	Overcast, cold, occasional heavy showers.

Activity B

1 Draw a diagram of a warm front. Write on your diagram the names of the clouds.

2 Imagine that the fronts are passing over you. List the clouds that you would see, in the order you would see them.

Hurricane Fury

Great Britain's weather may seem very changeable, but it is not often dangerous.

In other parts of the world, different weather patterns can seriously threaten or **hazard** life and property on a large scale. These types of weather include hurricanes, droughts, blizzards and tornadoes, and they can cause **natural disasters**. Avalanches, landslides, locust plagues, soil erosion and floods are not weather events, but they are often caused by them and result in serious damage.

HMS *Fife* was sent to the West Indian Islands in August, 1979 to help after a hurricane devastated the area. The letter is from a sailor on the ship, and is an eyewitness account of the effects of the hurricane.

Notes: The final death toll on Dominica was 57. Hurricane David continued towards the mainland passing over Haiti and the Dominican Republic where it caused over 2,000 deaths and made 200,000 people homeless.

Hurricane Frederic passed by Dominica, but caused more damage to the Dominican Republic and Haiti. When it reached the USA it was called 'the most costly ever' causing over £45 million damage in the city of Mobile alone.

photo 18: (Satellite of Hurricane Elena 2/9/85)

Activity A

1 Refer back to the fig 12 (diagram of Beaufort Scale of winds) on page 12. What speed in kilometres per hour must the wind blow at to be described as a hurricane?

2 Imagine you were part of a television team sent to cover the disaster on Dominica. Prepare a news bulletin. You could interview:

a the Prime Minister of the Island, Mr Oliver Saraphin, after he'd seen the devastation from HMS *Fife*'s helicopter.

b Chief Petty Officer Laughton, in charge of the distribution of supplies.

c a doctor in Princess Margaret's Hospital, who warns against drinking impure water.

d a police officer, warning looters.

Roseau
Dominica
3-7-79

Dear Peter,

At last I've found time to write to you. We struggled through stormy seas and gales to get here last Thursday. If that was the tail end of Hurricane David I'm glad we did not have to face its full fury!

The scene at Roseau, the island's capital, is terrible. There wasn't a building with a roof on! People were wandering around in shock. Even the Princess Margaret Hospital had been damaged by the 150 m.p.h. winds. There was no electricity, no pure water, and no phones. That wasn't really surprising as every telephone pole had been blown down. Over 60,000 people (out of the total population of 81,000) are thought to be homeless, at least 4,000 are injured. We know of 37 deaths, but expect the total to be higher. Lieut. Lipplett said it was just like the aftermath of a nuclear explosion.

We've rigged a canvas roof for the hospital, and got the power supply working. I've been down to the airport helping the chief petty officer organise the distribution of food and medicines. Our helicopter has been flying round the clock. It developed an oil leak on Sunday but we've not had time to fix it.

The people here are stunned. Most have lost their homes. Their livelihood is threatened too. Over three quarters of the banana crop has been destroyed. Today we were told of another hurricane coming this way. This is Hurricane Frederic.

Best wishes,
Bob.

Hurricanes can cause great damage because of the strong winds and the floods and storm waves which they help to cause. In 1900, one which passed over the West Indies and hit Galveston in Texas caused the death of nearly 6,000 people. The table shows some of the most damaging hurricanes in the last 30 years to affect the islands and coastlines of North America.

1957	Audrey	£150 million damage, 390 people killed.
1960	Donna	50 lives lost and £380 million damage.
1961	Carla	killed 46 people, damage of over £400 million.
1965	Betsey	75 people died, £1,400 million damage.
1969	Camille	256 lives lost and £1,400 million damage.
1972	Agnes	damage of over £2,000 million, 122 people died.
1979	Frederic	only 5 people killed, but damage estimated at £2,300 million.

fig 33

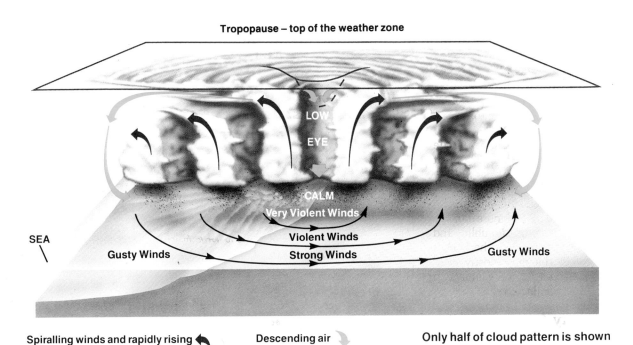

Tropopause – top of the weather zone

LOW

EYE

CALM
Very Violent Winds

Violent Winds

Strong Winds

SEA

Gusty Winds

Gusty Winds

Spiralling winds and rapidly rising moist air

Descending air

Only half of cloud pattern is shown

The weather conditions inside a hurricane are shown in fig 33. There is a calm **eye** in the centre of the storm. Around it is a mass of swirling, towering rainclouds with very strong and violent winds. The storm has massive amounts of energy, the air rises very fast and this causes very intense rainfall. The hurricane moves across the ocean quickly, taking only a few hours to pass over a place, but leaving a trail of destruction behind it. When the hurricane crosses on to land it soon begins to lose much of its energy. The wind speeds begin to drop and the swirl of cloud and rain turns into the more usual patterns of cloud and rain.

Activity B
1 Study the information about hurricanes.
a which killed nearly 6,000 people?
b when did Hurricane Donna come?
c what effect did Hurricane Audrey have?
d which two hurricanes did the most damage?
2 Write out a list of the amount of damage done by the seven hurricanes. What do you notice about the figures?

3 Compared with 1900, what do you notice about the number of lives lost in the more recent hurricanes?
4 What three features of hurricanes and their associated effects are responsible for most of the damage?
5 Find out from your school or public library how hurricanes in North America are named.

Facing the Hurricane

It is now possible to give advance warning of a hurricane; in the United States there are two levels:
- **hurricane watch** there is a 50% chance of a hurricane in the next 36 hours
- **hurricane warning** a hurricane is expected within the next 12 hours

This advice is given to people as soon as **hurricane watch** is announced:
- stay close to radio and television, listen to all news and weather bulletins
- store enough drinking water for three days
- store three days' supply of food, remember that normal electricity and gas supplies may not exist
- have emergency lighting such as paraffin lamps or candles
- reinforce and secure windows, doors, roofs, and any other loose fitments
- keep with you a first aid kit, a suitcase with overnight things and emergency food rations
- be prepared to move out of the area
- shelter during the hurricane, take all precaution you can against fire
- keep calm

Activity

1 Draw a map to show the paths of hurricanes.
a which parts of which oceans do not have many hurricanes?
b which two coastlines have most hurricane damage?
c what is there about the shape of these coastlines which might help explain this?
2 Hurricanes are given different names in different places, such as typhoon, willy-willy, tropical cyclone. Try to find out where each name is commonly used.
3 Design a poster to show the hurricane precaution code.

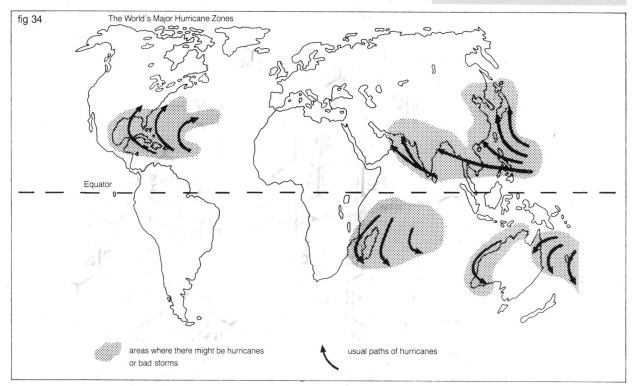

fig 34   The World's Major Hurricane Zones

Equator

areas where there might be hurricanes or bad storms

usual paths of hurricanes

Rules of the Hurricane Game

This game shows what happens when a hurricane passes over a place. To play you need: copies of the booking sheet, a copy of the board fig 35 and a die. Track your route across the board either by drawing it on or by moving a counter. You may play the game by yourself or with other players.

Throw the die. This will determine the **direction** you move: if you throw a **1** you move to the square on the left; if you throw a **5** or a **6** you move to the square on the right; and any **other** number you move straight ahead. The directions are shown in the key on the board. At each place there is:
- an arrow showing the direction of the wind
- a number showing the speed of the wind
- a letter referring to the amount of damage caused by the hurricane

Record each of these on the booking sheet.

When you reach the far side of the board total the amount of damage that you have had.

Each throw of the die represents one hour. A hurricane travels at about 14 – 24 km/hr. Inside it, the winds change in direction and speed, so that as the hurricane passes over, there will be more damage in some places than in others. Where the buildings are stronger, and the people more prepared, there will be even less damage.

The figures used in the game are only meant to give some idea of the situation, and are not to be taken literally.

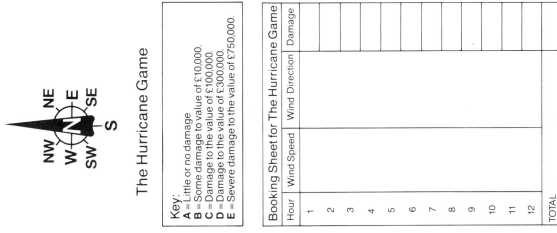

The Hurricane Game

Key:
A = Little or no damage
B = Some damage to value of £10,000.
C = Damage to the value of £100,000.
D = Damage to the value of £300,000.
E = Severe damage to the value of £750,000.

Booking Sheet for The Hurricane Game

Hour	Wind Speed	Wind Direction	Damage
1			
2			
3			
4			
5			
6			
7			
8			
9			
10			
11			
12			
TOTAL			

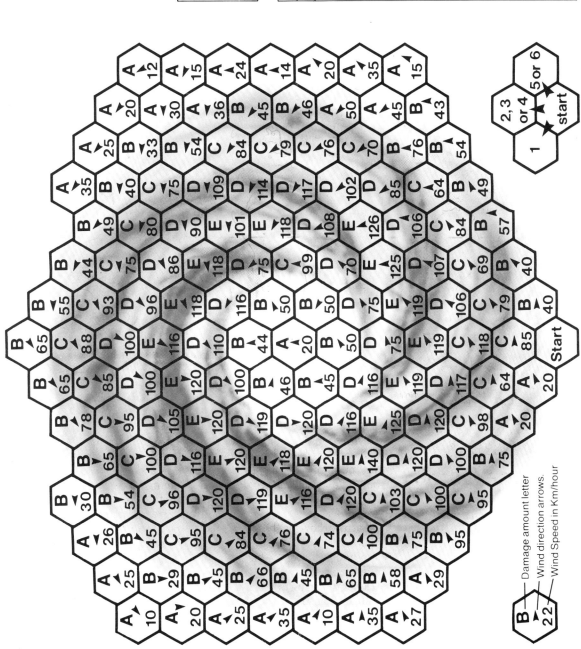

fig 35

When the rains fail . . .?

The spectacular, sudden, violent weather of a hurricane is one kind of weather extreme; weather can cause problems during periods when it seems quiet. Not enough rainfall or **drought**, can cause major difficulties for farmers, especially when it happens unexpectedly. Farmers need to be aware of weather patterns over a long period and plan their use of land and their farming work accordingly.

A rainfall pattern that is so **variable** makes forecasting the time when rain comes and the amount that falls very difficult.

One region where rainfall is variable is the Great Plains of the USA.

Here there are three main types of agricultural land use:

● the drier western areas of the Plains are used for grazing livestock
● in some places on drier land crops are grown. This is because the water from the rivers and wells can be used. This is called **irrigation**
● the eastern parts of the Plains have more rainfall and land is used to grow wheat and other crops. This is known as **arable farming**

photo 19: Great Plains farming

Activity A

1 Look at fig 36. Use your atlas to find the following:
a the latitude of the USA/Canada border.
b the state boundary which lies on longitude 100°W.
c the names of the ten states in which the Great Plains lie.
2 Make a careful copy of the map. Add to the key the names of the mountain range, rivers and towns.
3 Look at fig 37.
a state the amount of rain each year, and the seasonal pattern of rain in the Great Plains.
b how do the mean monthly temperatures vary throughout the year?
4 Look at photo 19. Describe in three or four sentences what the scenery is like.

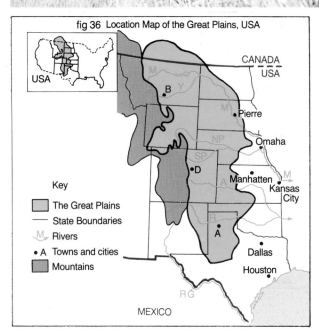

fig 36 Location Map of the Great Plains, USA

CANADA
USA
USA
B Y
• Pierre
• Omaha
• D
Manhatten
Kansas City
• A
• Dallas
Houston
RG
MEXICO

Key

The Great Plains
State Boundaries
Rivers
• A Towns and cities
Mountains

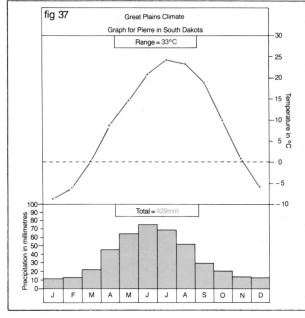

fig 37

Great Plains Climate

Graph for Pierre in South Dakota

Range = 33°C

Total = 429mm

Temperature in °C

Precipitation in millimetres

J F M A M J J A S O N D

Farms and ranches throughout the Plains have some things in common:
● most are very large
● a lot of modern machinery is used
● they do not employ many people
● they are highly productive

Although farms are successful and prosperous in the Great Plains today, this was not always the case. During the 1930s there was a period of several years of prolonged drought in the Great Plains. The winds blew away great clouds of topsoil from the land. This dust hid the sun, buried farmhouses, suffocated people and led to a natural disaster. The situation was made worse because at the same time there was an economic disaster called the **Great Depression**. This meant that the value of farm products dropped dramatically.

Black Sunday was the name given in the Great Plains to the day of April 14th, 1935. Stratford in Northern Texas was one of many of the towns hit by a dust storm and one Texas schoolboy described his experiences:

These storms were like rolling black smoke. We had to keep the lights on all day. We went to school with the headlights on and wearing dust masks. You could hardly tell the difference between day and night.

photo 20: A tractor becoming buried by the dust

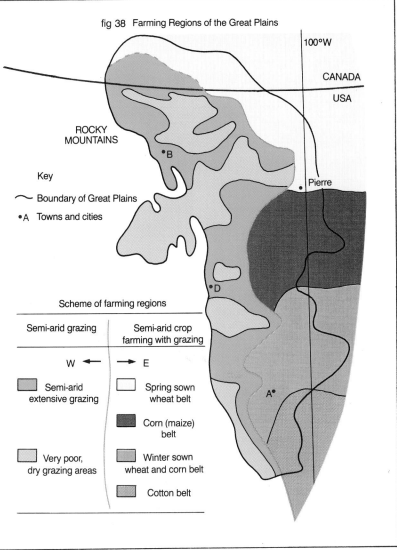

fig 38   Farming Regions of the Great Plains

100°W

CANADA

USA

ROCKY MOUNTAINS

•B

•Pierre

Key

— Boundary of Great Plains
•A   Towns and cities

•D

•A

Scheme of farming regions

Semi-arid grazing	Semi-arid crop farming with grazing
W ←	→ E
▨ Semi-arid extensive grazing	▢ Spring sown wheat belt
	▨ Corn (maize) belt
▢ Very poor, dry grazing areas	▨ Winter sown wheat and corn belt
	▨ Cotton belt

photo 21: Dust in the street

Vast numbers of people became so desperate that they left their farms and homes, and migrated to places like California.

Activity B

Use your school or public library to find out about the periods of droughts in the Great Plains. You should look for references about the **Dust Bowl**. Try to find eye-witness accounts of what it was like.

A drought happens when for a number of years the rainfall is less than the expected average.

• the lower of the two graphs in fig 39 shows the drought in the 1930s when the Dust Bowl occurred. This was the worst drought since 1600 AD but it is part of a pattern of wetter and drier periods

• the top graph shows the amount of wheat harvested per hectare, rising and falling in wetter and drier periods. The average wheat yield has risen as farming methods have improved, but it still varies year by year

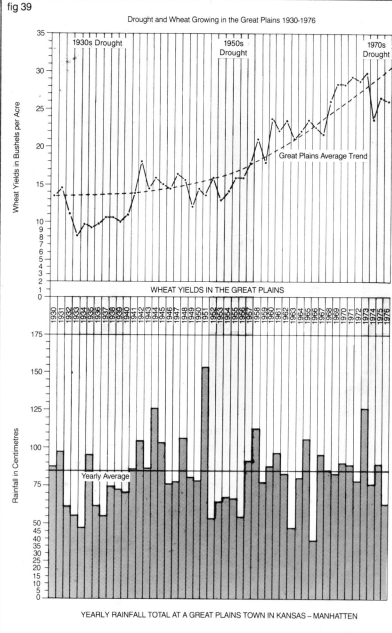

fig 39

Drought and Wheat Growing in the Great Plains 1930-1976

WHEAT YIELDS IN THE GREAT PLAINS

YEARLY RAINFALL TOTAL AT A GREAT PLAINS TOWN IN KANSAS – MANHATTEN

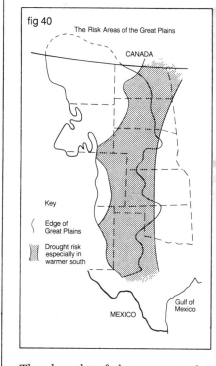

fig 40

The Risk Areas of the Great Plains

Key

Edge of Great Plains

Drought risk especially in warmer south

CANADA

MEXICO

Gulf of Mexico

The drought of the 1930s in the Great Plains was not the only reason for the devastation of the land. At that time farming methods were not suited to the climate of the region. The **Dust Bowl** was a result of these events:

• much of the planted crop had withered and died and so was useless

• bare, exposed soil was blown away by the winds

• new vegetation could not grow because the fine top soil containing the plant foods had blown away

• unprotected sub-soil wore down into deep channels or **gullies** on the occasions it did rain

• much of the land became useless, the farmers had earned no money and they were forced to move

The two-stage removal of the soil is called **soil erosion**. First the top soil is removed by wind, next the sub soil is removed by rain. Soil erosion happens all the time, but normally when it does occur new soil is formed to replace the eroded soil. During the drought soil erosion was so serious that no new soil could form to replace that worn away.

Activity A

1 Study fig 39 and then answer these questions:

a what is the average rainfall for the town of Manhatten, Kansas?

b what was the rainfall in the following years?
1934   1951   1954   1968   1976.

c what are the dates of the periods of drought?

d was the yield of wheat above or below average in these years?

e are the yields of wheat above or below average in the periods between the droughts?

f why do you think this is so?

g why does the average wheat yield increase throughout this period?

Managing with little rain

The Dust Bowl of the 1930s has not happened again. There have been periods of drought, but with the help of the United States Government farmers do not need to depend so much on one year's harvest. The Government has given financial help and built large scale irrigation schemes. Research and advice about farming methods have meant that techniques have changed. Modern farming includes:

- growing a wider range of drought resistant crops
- irrigation
- ploughing across slopes to avoid soil moving downhill
- re-seeding of grasslands
- preserving moisture in the soil
- using manure or fertilizers

The problem of variable rainfall has been overcome, but only with modern technology, financial assistance and an active government willing to plan the campaign with people who understand the problem. There are many other areas of the world where drought is a very serious problem, and the difficulties are still there today, such as Ethiopia 1984 – 5. Can the solutions to the problems of the Dust Bowl be applied to poorer countries?

Activity B
1 Draw a chart with two columns. Call the chart Modern Methods of Farming in the Great Plains; call the first column Farmers' Actions and the second column Government Help. In each column list the modern solutions to the problems caused by the variable rainfall of the Great Plains.
2 Describe the photographs on this page.
3 How can the people in rich countries help poorer countries, such as Ethiopia, overcome the disastrous effects of drought?

photo 22: Hoover dam

photo 23: Contour farming

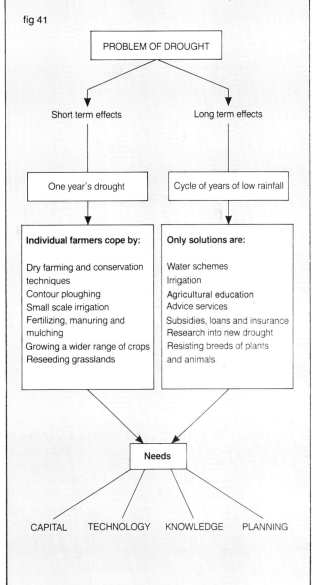

fig 41

PROBLEM OF DROUGHT

Short term effects | Long term effects

One year's drought | Cycle of years of low rainfall

Individual farmers cope by:

Dry farming and conservation techniques
Contour ploughing
Small scale irrigation
Fertilizing, manuring and mulching
Growing a wider range of crops
Reseeding grasslands

Only solutions are:

Water schemes
Irrigation
Agricultural education
Advice services
Subsidies, loans and insurance
Research into new drought
Resisting breeds of plants
and animals

Needs

CAPITAL   TECHNOLOGY   KNOWLEDGE   PLANNING

Planet Earth

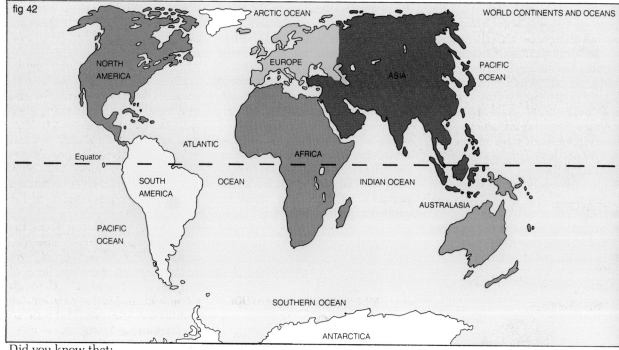

fig 42   WORLD CONTINENTS AND OCEANS

ARCTIC OCEAN

NORTH AMERICA

EUROPE

ASIA

PACIFIC OCEAN

ATLANTIC

Equator

AFRICA

SOUTH AMERICA

OCEAN

INDIAN OCEAN

AUSTRALASIA

PACIFIC OCEAN

SOUTHERN OCEAN

ANTARCTICA

Did you know that:
- the earth is not a perfect sphere, it is widest at the equator (12,756 km diameter) and shortest at the poles (12,714 km diameter)
- a journey round the equator is 40,076 km
- the earth spins once every 23 hrs 56 mins and 4 secs
- 71% of the earth's surface is covered by oceans
- seven large land masses called continents cover the remaining 29%
- the difference between the highest point of land (Mount Everest at 8,848 m) and the deepest part of the ocean (the Marianas Trench at 11,035 m) is small compared to the size of the earth

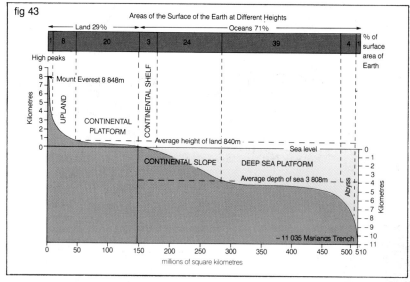

fig 43   Areas of the Surface of the Earth at Different Heights

Land 29%   Oceans 71%

| 8 | 20 | 3 | 24 | 39 | 4 | 1 | % of surface area of Earth |

High peaks

Mount Everest 8 848m

UPLAND

CONTINENTAL PLATFORM

CONTINENTAL SHELF

Average height of land 840m

Sea level

CONTINENTAL SLOPE

DEEP SEA PLATFORM

Average depth of sea 3 808m

Abyss

−11 035 Marianas Trench

millions of square kilometres

Activity A

1 On a map of the world:

a mark and name the following lines of latitude: the Equator, the Tropics of Cancer and Capricorn, and the Arctic and Antarctic Circles.

b colour and name each continent.

c mark on these two lines of longitude: the Greenwich or Prime Meridian (0°) and the International Date Line (180°).

2 Use your atlas to find out which continent:

a contains the Himalayan Mountains.

b has no permanent settlement.

c contains the city that hosted the 1984 Olympics.

d contains the least number of countries.

e has no land outside of latitude 40°S and 40°N.

f has the largest population.

g you live in.

h contains the Amazon Forest and Pampas Grasslands.

i has the River Ganges flowing across it.

j contains the Atacama Desert.

3 Look at fig 43.

a what is the difference in height between the highest land and deepest ocean?

b what is the average height of the land?

c what is the average depth of the oceans?

d what is the true edge of the continents?

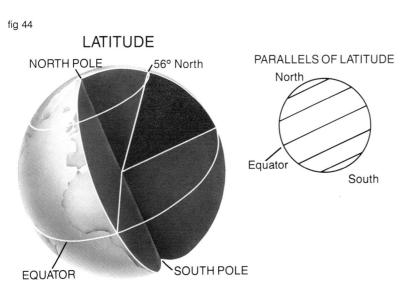

fig 44

LATITUDE

NORTH POLE
56° North

PARALLELS OF LATITUDE

North

Equator

South

EQUATOR
SOUTH POLE

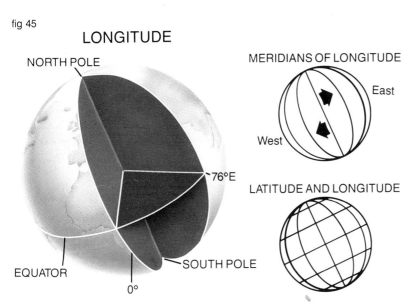

fig 45

LONGITUDE

NORTH POLE

MERIDIANS OF LONGITUDE

East

West

76°E

LATITUDE AND LONGITUDE

EQUATOR
SOUTH POLE

0°

The lines drawn on the surface of a globe are imaginary lines. They are called lines of **latitude** and **longitude**, and are used on maps to find the position of a place. They are particularly useful where there are few recognisable features, such as at sea.

The latitude of a place shows how far north or south of the equator it is. Lines of latitude are parallel and numbered in degrees north or south from the equator (see fig 44). Your atlas will show on a map of Great Britain that Newcastle upon Tyne is on a latitude line numbered 55°N. This means that it has a latitudinal position 55 degrees north of the equator.

Lines of longitude run from the North Pole to the South Pole and cross all lines of latitude at right angles (see fig 45). The lines of longitude running through Greenwich in London is given the longitude of 0 degrees. This is called the **Greenwich Meridian**. All other places are given their longitudinal position in degrees east or west of this line. Newcastle upon Tyne is shown in your atlas to be just more than 1 degree west of the Greenwich Meridian. Since each degree can be divided up into 60 parts called minutes, it can be worked out as 1 degree 35 minutes west.

The position of a place is where imaginary lines of latitude and longitude cross, so Newcastle upon Tyne has a position of latitude 55°N, longitude 1° 35′W.

photo 24

Activity B

1 Use the index in your atlas to find the latitudes of the following towns and cities in North America and Great Britain: New Orleans, Minneapolis, Los Angeles, Philadelphia, Harrogate and Falkirk.

2 Find an atlas map of North America. What is the latitude of the long straight part of the Canada-USA border?

3 Study an atlas map of Europe. Name 2 large cities found at latitude 60°N and 4 large cities found at 50°N.

4 Give the longitude in degrees of Berwick upon Tweed in England, Hamburg in West Germany and Pittsburgh and New York in the USA.

5 Give the full positions in latitude and longitude of London, Cardiff, Belfast and Edinburgh in Great Britain and San Francisco, Winnipeg, Mexico City and Chicago in North America.

6 Define latitude, longitude and Greenwich Meridian in your dictionary.

In the north west of America, in a mountain range called the Cascades is a sacred mountain known to the Indians as

LOOWIT
The Lady of Fire
They worshipped the fire God of the mountain...

...but the White men who moved into the area after 1850 renamed the mountain. They called it...

But...in 1978 two scientists wrote a report on their studies of the mountain...

...Mount St. Helens. The beautiful area was reserved for holiday makers, foresters and hunters.

IT SAYS HERE 'THE MOUNTAIN WILL PROBABLY ERUPT BEFORE THE END OF THIS CENTURY.'

YES, AND IT ADDS THAT THE ERUPTION WILL BE VIOLENT!'

So Mount St. Helens was watched carefully...

QUICK! WE MUST SEE THE STATE GOVERNOR-

THE MOUNTAIN HAS HAD OVER 47 EARTHQUAKES AND NOW HAS A CRATER 70 METRES ACROSS AND A BULGE ON THE NORTHSIDE!

WHAT'S UP OFFICER?

SORRY SIR, NO ONE IS ALLOWED UP THE MOUNTAIN. THIS IS A RESTRICTED AREA. IT MIGHT BLOW ANY TIME!

Some like Geologist Dave Johnston

remained to work and observe...

Some like 84-year-old Harry Trueman refused to move.

NO ONE KNOWS MORE ABOUT THIS MOUNTAIN THAN ME, AND IT DON'T DARE BLOW UP ON ME!

AND I'M NOT LEAVING MY 16 CATS!

At 7.00 a.m. Geologists Keith and Dorothy Stoffel board a light plane at Yakima Airport to make a reconnaissance flight . . .

At 8.32 they were directly over the mountain, when . . .

KEITH.....LOOK AT THAT!!

The Stoffels both survived . . . Others weren't so lucky . . .

VANCOUVER! VANCOUVER! THIS IS IT......

THE MOUNTAIN! ITS GONE! TURN SOUTH! FULL THROTTLE.... QUICK.

That was the last message received from Dave Johnston.

Rescue teams moved in quickly.

A STRANGE MOON LIKE LANDSCAPE WITH ALL THIS GREY ASH AND DUST.

OVER HALF THE MOUNTAINSIDE HAS GONE.

NO SIGN OF HARRY TRUEMAN'S LODGE.

THAT BRINGS DEATH TOLL TO 61. WE'VE RESCUED 198.

NO ONE ALIVE HERE, EITHER!

LOOK AT ALL THOSE TREES, SNAPPED OFF LIKE MATCH STICKS.

THE BLAST RELEASED 500 TIMES MORE ENERGY THAN THE A-BOMB DROPPED ON HIROSHIMA!

And so LOOWIT the Lady of Fire returned to life – its first volcanic eruption for 123 years!

VOLCANO BLOWS UP

Gigantic Ash Cloud

Airline Pilot's View of The Awesome Display

An airline pilot flying near the Mount St. Helens volcano when it erupted yesterday morning described the clouds that belched out of the volcano as "the biggest I've ever seen".

"It was a huge, greyish-black mushroom cloud", said Captain Joe Mathes, a United Airlines pilot who saw the explosion from 35,000 feet.

The captain, crew and 68 passengers on the Los Angeles-to-Seattle flight watched the cloud "boil up to about 60,000 feet", Mathes said.

"It was different from the normal cloud", the airline captain told *The Chronicle*. "It was greyish black and extremely dense — the sun couldn't shine through. The cloud was about 35 miles in diameter."

Mathes said he saw "lightning flash in there". The eruption created its own weather — "and it cast a shadow easily 60 miles to the north-west".

Vancouver. Wash.

Mount St. Helens burst into a frenzied eruption yesterday with a shattering blast that rocked thousands of square miles of the Pacific Northwest, killed at least five persons, lofted a boiling, black cloud of ash 12 miles into the stratosphere, flooded nearby streams and washed out several bridges.

Winds carried ash to the east for hundreds of miles, covering areas within 50 miles with up to a half inch of volcanic debris.

The awesome display, coming as the volcano 40 miles northeast of here seemed to have settled down after eight weeks of fitful activity, began with an earthquake and massive explosion from the mountain's summit and north flank at 8.32 a.m.

The quake, measuring 5.0 on the Richter Scale, was easily the most severe seismic disturbance since Mount St. Helens began erupting March 27, its first activity in 123 years.

The roar sent shock waves for hundreds of miles. "Our house was just shaking, and it sounded like artillery", said Jay Collins of Bellingham, Wash., 200 miles away.

There were no confirmed sightings of molten lava bubbling from the volcano —experts say volcanoes such as Mount St. Helens seldom produce lava — but mudflows raced down the flanks of the 9,000-plus-foot mountain and flooded the south fork of the nearby Toutle River, washing out several bridges on the Spirit Lake Highway.

In the late afternoon there was a continuous, dark grey stream of pyroclastics — a mixture of superheated gas, dust and volcanic ash — spurting from the top of the mountain.

The 1,000-degree Fahrenheit mixture was flowing steadily from the top at speeds estimated up to 80 miles an hour, according to Carolyn Driedger, a Tacoma, Wash., geologist who works for the U.S. Geological Survey.

The crater at the summit grew to at least half a mile in diameter, and its rim dropped 500 to 600 feet below Mount St. Helens' pre-eruption height of 9,677 feet. The timberline is at 5,000 feet.

Inside a Volcano

On the 18th May 1980 Mount St. Helens erupted. It was much more violent than scientists had anticipated. This eruption was only the most recent of many which have happened in the north west USA over thousands of years. There are many volcanoes and lava flows in this area, particularly around the Cascade mountains.

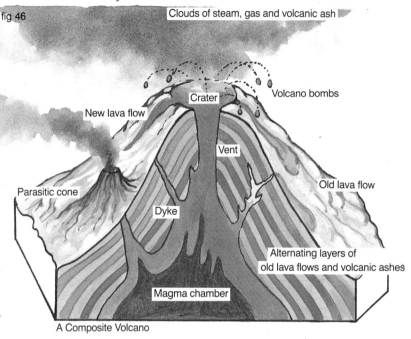

fig 46

Clouds of steam, gas and volcanic ash

Volcano bombs

Crater

New lava flow

Vent

Old lava flow

Parasitic cone

Dyke

Alternating layers of old lava flows and volcanic ashes

Magma chamber

A Composite Volcano

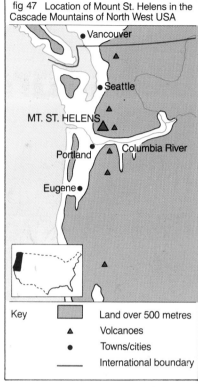

fig 47 Location of Mount St. Helens in the Cascade Mountains of North West USA

Vancouver

Seattle

MT. ST. HELENS

Portland

Columbia River

Eugene

Key — Land over 500 metres
▲ Volcanoes
• Towns/cities
—— International boundary

Mount St. Helens is an example of one type of volcano. It is called a **composite cone** because it is made up of layers of volcanic ash and lava. **Volcanic ash** is fine dust and debris which erupts with steam and gases from the explosion. **Lava** is molten rock coming from a large **magma chamber** underneath the volcano. It is forced upward by pressure through channels and **vents** connected with the surface. When the volcano explodes it sometimes forms a **crater** in the surface through which the lava can flow.

When a composite cone erupts it usually produces some ash followed by lava. After many eruptions the volcano has alternating layers, as shown in fig 46. The shape may be quite complicated. It depends on the cracks in the volcano that the lava follows to reach the surface forming **dykes** and **parasite cones**.

Activity

1 Read the newspaper account and then
a describe what the photograph shows.
b list from the journalist's account eight features of the eruption and its effects on the surrounding land.
2 Write a story about the eruption using the newspaper account and the cartoon on pages 32 and 33.
3 Why do composite cones have alternating layers of ash and lava?
4 Make a cut-out model of a composite volcano.
5 Find out examples of famous volcanoes of the composite type.

photo 25: Lava flow

photo 26: Old lava flow

Different Volcanoes

photo 27: Paracutin

Dionisio Pulido was ploughing at 4 am on 20th February 1943 when a crack appeared in the field where he was working. The ground swelled up by about two metres, smoke and a fine grey dust came out; there was a smell of sulphur. The ground shook and trembled. Dionisio fled back to the village in terror. Later that day some people from a nearby town found the hole and saw ashes, sparks and dust being thrown into the air. When the volcano ceased to erupt nine years later in 1952 the cone was over 400 metres high. Dionisio's village of Paracutin and the nearby town of San Juan de Parangaricutio were buried. This volcano is an example of an **ash cone**.

The island of Hawaii is made up of five sea floor volcanoes which have been built up above sea level by lava flows over millions of years. The largest of them, Mauna Loa, is actually a mountain of over 8,615 m, but only the top 4,207 m is above sea level. It erupted in 1984 giving out a runny, flowing lava. It is a wide gently sloping **shield volcano** which is 112 km wide at the base, with an average slope of 4 to 5 degrees.

The volcanoes of Hawaii are continually erupting and are therefore called **active**. This is not usual, most volcanoes are sleeping or **dormant** because they only erupt after long periods of time. Edinburgh Castle is built on the remains of a large volcano. The only part left is the plug of the original vent of the volcano. This 'dead' volcano is **extinct**.

fig 48

TYPES OF VOLCANIC ACTIVITY ON THE SURFACE OF THE CRUST

- EXPLOSION → COMBINED LAVA FLOWS AND EXPLOSIONS ← FLOWS OF LAVA

	Giant collapsed craters	Alternate layers of ash and lava	Very runny lava from a long line of vents or fissures	Runny lava from a central vent	Sticky lava from a central vent
Cinder or ash cone	**Caldera**	**Composite volcano**	**Lava plateau**	**Shield volcano**	**Acid lava dome**
e.g. Paracutin	e.g. Vesuvius Krakatoa	e.g. Mount Fuji Mount St. Helens	e.g. Antrim Plateau	e.g. Mauna Loa	

→ Long erosion of any of these when extinct may leave part of the old vent or plug

Volcano neck

e.g. Edinburgh and Stirling Castle Rocks

photo 28: Mauna Loa

photo 29: Edinburgh's volcanic plug

Activity A

Imagine you are a TV newsreader. Plan a news item to read out, with diagrams, about your chosen eruption.

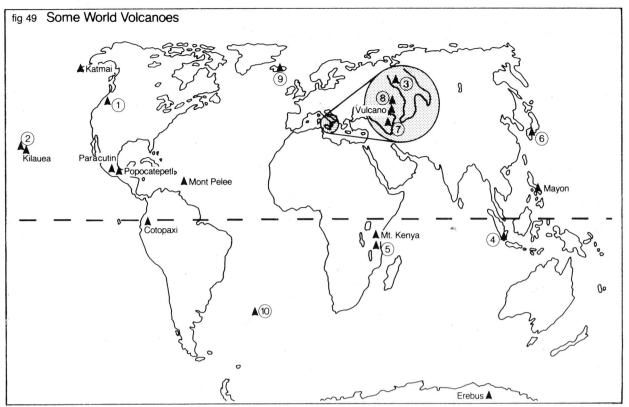

fig 49   **Some World Volcanoes**

Volcanoes are not found in all parts of the world. The ones marked on the map can be grouped in certain zones:

● Erebus, Krakatoa, Mayon, Fuji, Katmai and Mount St. Helens are in the Pacific Ring of Fire
● Mont Pelee, Tristan da Cunha, Mauna Loa, Hekla and Kilauea are in the oceans
● Vesuvius and Etna are in or near the Mediterranean sea
● Kilimanjaro and Mount Kenya are along the East African Rift valley

Volcanoes are distributed in a definite pattern, some areas are much more likely to have volcanoes than others. There is something about the structure of the earth in these areas which could explain this.

Activity B

1 The puzzle contains the names of volcanoes on the world map.

a find the twenty named volcanoes and list them.

b the remaining letters spell out a message. When you have worked this out in rough, write the three sentences neatly in your book after the volcano list.

c use the list and your atlas to complete the message.

2 Copy the map.

a colour in and name each of the volcanic zones separately.

b fill in the names of all the volcanoes on the map using an atlas.

c find the latitude and longitude of any 10 of the volcanoes using the atlas index.

3 Research one volcanic eruption for a project work, using your local library.

T	H	M	O	U	N	T	K	E	N	Y	A	E	A	N	T	E	S	K	S
E	T	K	I	L	I	M	A	N	J	A	R	O	W	M	E	N	T	R	U
P	Y	V	O	L	C	A	N	O	E	S	A	S	R	A	E	A	M	A	B
C	O	T	O	P	A	X	I	O	N	G	N	T	S	U	T	T	H	K	E
E	M	P	O	S	T	F	A	M	O	E	U	R	N	N	S	I	N	A	R
T	H	E	O	W	O	R	L	D	L	T	E	O	N	A	O	E	F	T	E
T	H	E	M	C	A	R	E	E	F	O	Y	M	U	L	N	E	D	O	S
U	H	E	K	L	A	R	H	R	O	A	U	B	N	O	D	L	I	A	F
P	A	R	I	C	U	T	I	N	M	N	G	O	T	A	H	E	E	P	U
A	C	I	F	I	S	C	E	O	C	E	A	L	N	I	N	P	A	B	J
E	L	K	A	T	M	A	I	P	T	C	A	I	L	L	E	T	D	T	I
H	E	P	N	A	C	I	F	V	E	S	U	V	I	U	S	N	I	C	R
I	V	U	L	C	A	N	O	N	G	T	O	F	F	I	R	U	E	A	L
I	O	S	T	O	F	T	H	E	K	I	L	A	U	E	A	O	S	E	T
M	T	R	I	S	T	A	N	D	A	C	U	N	H	A	E	M	N	I	S

'Quake hits 'Frisco

April 18th 1906 dawned with a light early mist for the half a million people of San Francisco, California. The forecast was for another clear sunny day for the bustling city. It turned out to be the most catastrophic day in the city's history:

- at 5.13 am there was a minor earth tremor, it lasted for over a minute, but people were used to these
- at 5.15 am a deep rumbling came and then a violent **earthquake** struck; it lasted for just over 2½ mins
- there was a deafening roar of collapsing buildings. Roads buckled and heaved as shock waves ran through the ground. A sound of church bells was set off afterwards by the shaking earth
- the earthquake caused £20 million of damage. Besides the damage to the ground itself gas and oil pipes had broken, electric cables were down and sparking wildly, stoves were overturned and chimneys brought down. Fires burnt over the city especially where the houses were built of wood
- it was difficult to stop the fires: the streets were blocked and the main water pipes fractured, so there was no water
- the fires took hold and burned for three days and two nights. They covered an area six times bigger than the Great Fire of London in 1666. They caused damage costing twenty times as much as the earthquake and nearly 500 people died
- this earthquake occurred right across a giant weakness or **fault line** in the earth's crust called the San Andreas Fault, which covers this part of California. Although it only lasted 2½ mins, it caused an enormous amount of damage

photo 30: Flames and debris in California street

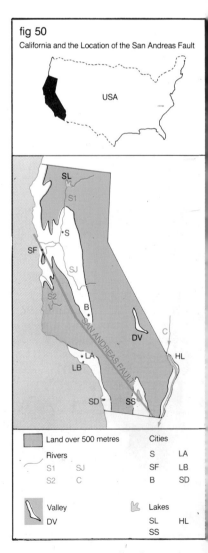

fig 50
California and the Location of the San Andreas Fault

USA

Land over 500 metres		Cities	
Rivers		S	LA
S1	SJ	SF	LB
S2	C	B	SD
Valley		Lakes	
DV		SL	HL
		SS	

Activity A

1 Draw a copy of the map in fig 50. Add the names of the towns and rivers using your atlas.
2 Answer these questions:
a how long did the first tremor last?
b at what time did the main earthquake strike?
c what damage was caused by this earthquake?
d what caused the most damage?
e why did the earthquake happen in this place?
f why did it start?
3 Design a newspaper front page for April 19th 1906. Imagine you were a reporter in San Francisco sending back your report to your paper in New York.

The San Andreas Fault

Scientists measure earthquakes with an instrument called a **seismograph**. This records the shock waves which travel in and through the rocks of the earth. A typical recording or seismogram looks like fig 51. An earthquake produces three groups of shock waves; the first two travel quickly within the body of the earth, but the last group cause the damage since they travel slowly acting like waves in the ground.

The records of the faster shock waves are collected from several seismographic recording stations and compared. This allows scientists to find out exactly where the earthquake started or the **focus** in the earth's crust. The shock waves travel outwards from the focus and cause most damage on the surface at the **epicentre**. Further away from this the shock waves lose energy and so the amount of damage decreases. Earthquakes occur along breaks or weaknesses in the earth's crust where there are movements, such as along the San Andreas fault. Earthquakes can also happen when a volcano erupts, this warns people of the eruption. In Mount St. Helens earthquakes occurred as molten magma moved upwards towards the surface. Minor earthquakes are more common than people realise.

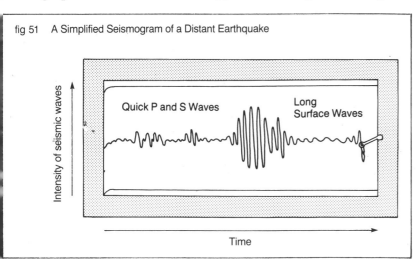

fig 51   A Simplified Seismogram of a Distant Earthquake

Intensity of seismic waves

Quick P and S Waves

Long Surface Waves

Time

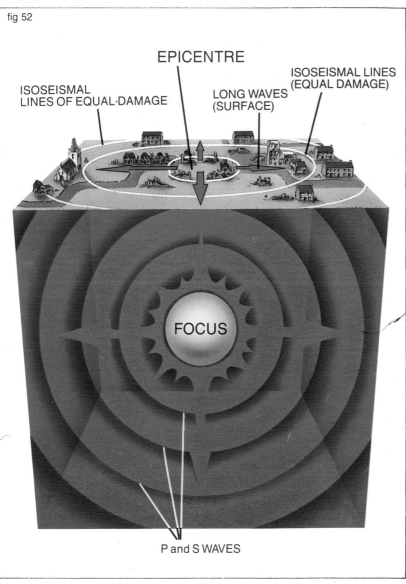

fig 52

EPICENTRE

ISOSEISMAL LINES OF EQUAL·DAMAGE

LONG WAVES (SURFACE)

ISOSEISMAL LINES (EQUAL DAMAGE)

FOCUS

P and S WAVES

Activity B

1 Draw a diagram showing the features of an earthquake.

2 Using this, and the text, copy out the following passage and fill in the missing words:

"An earthquake starts within the earth's crust at the . . . . . . The epicentre is . . . . above this on the earth's . . . . The shock waves are recorded by a scientist on a . . . . The records show . . . . . groups of waves. The first . . . travel within the earth, but the last group cause most . . . . . . because they travel on the . . . .

Earthquakes result from any movements within the earth's crust. Fault lines like . . . . are common locations, as are . . . . The amount of damage caused gets . . . . away from the epicentre."

Earthquake Patterns

fig 53 Richter's Scale of Earthquake Magnitude

Magnitude	Effects at epicentre	
1 to 3.4	None, only recorded on seismographs.	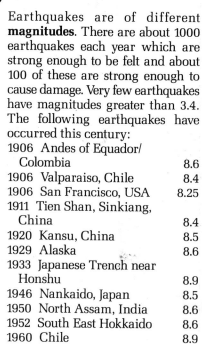
3.5 to 4.2	Feels like the vibrations due to a passing lorry. Notice by people at rest.	
4.3 to 4.8	Noticed by everyone. Loose objects are rocked, sleepers woken up and church bells ring.	
4.9 to 5.4	Trees sway, loose objects fall. Some damage.	
5.5 to 6.1	Walls crack, plaster falls. General alarm.	
6.2 to 6.9	Some buildings collapse. Chimneys fall. Pipes break. Ground fissured or cracked.	
7.0 to 7.3	Ground cracks badly. Buildings destroyed. Railway lines bent. Landslides.	
7.4 to 8.1	Only few buildings withstand shock, bridges destroyed. All pipes and cables broken, landslides, floods.	
over 8.1	Countryside devastated. Total destruction.	

Earthquakes are of different **magnitudes**. There are about 1000 earthquakes each year which are strong enough to be felt and about 100 of these are strong enough to cause damage. Very few earthquakes have magnitudes greater than 3.4. The following earthquakes have occurred this century:

1906 Andes of Equador/Colombia 8.6
1906 Valparaiso, Chile 8.4
1906 San Francisco, USA 8.25
1911 Tien Shan, Sinkiang, China 8.4
1920 Kansu, China 8.5
1929 Alaska 8.6
1933 Japanese Trench near Honshu 8.9
1946 Nankaido, Japan 8.5
1950 North Assam, India 8.6
1952 South East Hokkaido 8.6
1960 Chile 8.9
1964 Anchorage, Alaska 8.6
1977 North China 8.5
1985 Mexico 8.1

photo 31: San Francisco after the earthquake

In 1935 C. F. Richter worked out a way of comparing the magnitude of earthquakes. He used studies of Californian earthquakes along the San Andreas Fault in the USA to devise the **Richter scale**, this is now widely used around the world.

On this scale earthquakes of 3.4 and under are minor and while they can be detected by seismographs they do not produce effects that are normally noticed. In Britain earthquakes are usually minor ones. There was one in Colchester in 1884 of magnitude 6.9 but this did not cause large scale damage. Earthquakes have occurred recently in Wales but only with local alarm and minor damage to buildings. One of the most catastrophic earthquakes recorded was near the Japanese Trench close to the Island of Honshu, with a magnitude of 8.9.

The Richter scale measures the total amount of energy released at the epicentre. This means that each earthquake is only related to one reading on the scale. The amount of damage is measured by a scale of **intensity** invented by an Italian scientist, Mercalli. The intensity of an earthquake gets less the further it is from the epicentre this means each earthquake will have several readings on **Mercalli's scale**.

Much of the destruction is not due to the shock waves of the earthquake but to the after effects such as fire, floods or so-called tidal waves or **tsunamis**. For instance much of the destruction of San Francisco in 1906 resulted from fire.

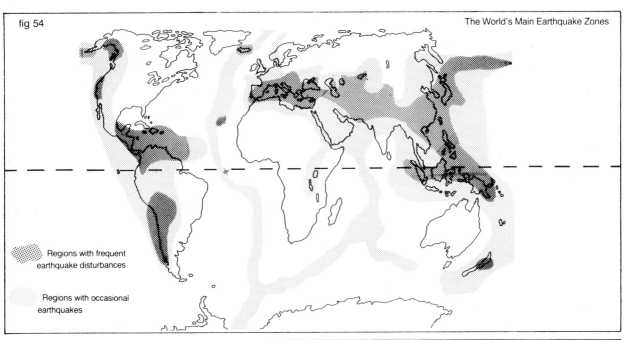

fig 54   The World's Main Earthquake Zones

Regions with frequent
earthquake disturbances

Regions with occasional
earthquakes

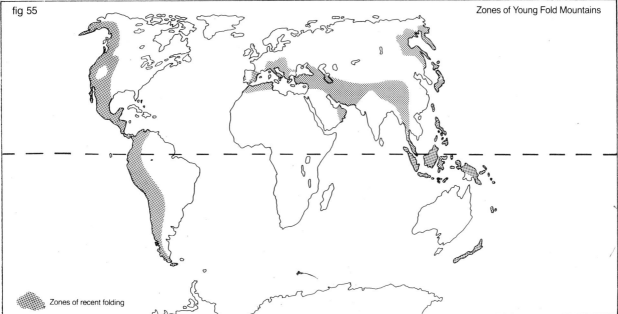

fig 55   Zones of Young Fold Mountains

Zones of recent folding

Earthquakes can happen anywhere, but as fig 54 shows they are most common:

- around the Pacific Ocean
- along the Mediterranean Sea coastlands into Southern Asia
- through the middle of the Atlantic, Indian and Southern Oceans

This grouping of earthquakes corresponds with the grouping of volcanoes and with the main mountain ranges. Scientists think these all result from movements in the earth's crust. The world's main **fold mountains** are formed by the buckling of rocks where the earth's crust has moved.

Activity

1 Look at the earthquake scale on page 40, and answer the following:
a what is the name of the scientist who worked out the scale of the magnitude of earthquakes?
b how are earthquakes under 3.5 detected?
c what was the magnitude of the 1964 Alaska earthquake?
d was this stronger or weaker than the San Francisco earthquake of 1906?
e where was the 1911 earthquake of magnitude 8.4?
f where and how strong were the most catastrophic earthquakes?
2 Add to your dictionary the following words and their meanings: epicentre, focus, magnitude, seismograph, Richter scale, tsunami, fault and fold mountain.
3 What is the difference between the magnitude and intensity of an earthquake?
4 Compare the distribution of volcanoes, earthquakes and fold mountains.

Moving Plates

The earth is a sphere, but with a surface rather like an egg with a cracked shell.

It has three main layers:
- a very hot **core** with a solid centre and liquid rock outside
- a thin **crust** of solid rock. The surface of the earth is made up of slabs of rock called **plates** composed mainly of crust. These float like rafts on the mantle, and can move at a few centimetres a year. The boundaries between these slabs or plates are shown on the map. Some of the plates are made of thin and dense material called oceanic crust. Others consist of thicker but lighter rocks of the continental crust.

The information needed to find out about these plates came from many different scientific studies. These included earthquake records and studies of the patterns of earthquakes, volcanoes and fold mountains. Many of these features are found or distributed in similar places, which we now know are the boundaries of the plates. However, not all fold mountains or extinct volcanoes are found on these boundaries. Perhaps the pattern of the plates has not always been the same.

fig 56

The Interior of the Earth

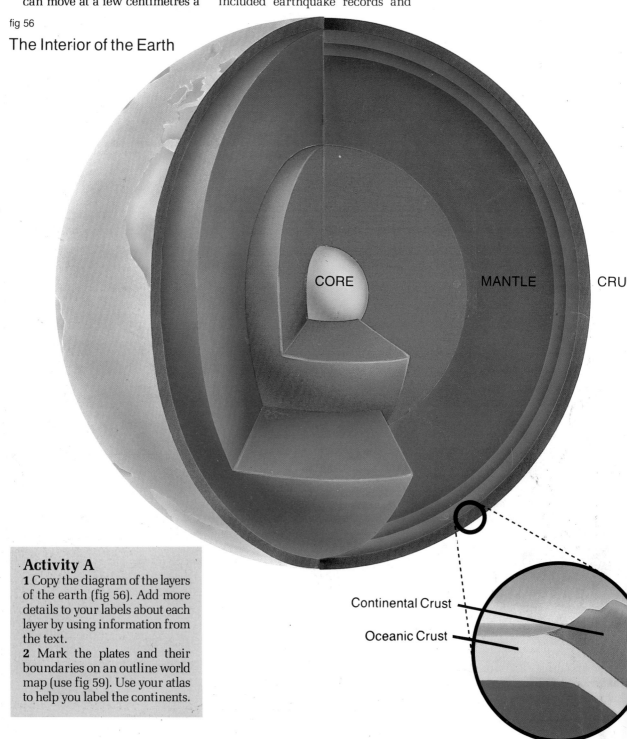

CORE MANTLE CRU

Continental Crust

Oceanic Crust

Activity A
1 Copy the diagram of the layers of the earth (fig 56). Add more details to your labels about each layer by using information from the text.
2 Mark the plates and their boundaries on an outline world map (use fig 59). Use your atlas to help you label the continents.

On the surface of the earth there is a lot of tension because the plates are moving.

Plates cause tension by:
- moving apart, this is called a **constructive** boundary
- moving together, this is called a **destructive** boundary

A constructive boundary is found in the middle of the Atlantic Ocean (see fig 57 and map). It is marked on the ocean floor by a line of volcanoes called a **mid-ocean ridge**. Here the mantle breaks through the crust and spreads out on the surface through volcanoes as lava. This pushes the plates apart by forming new crust on the ocean floor.

A destructive boundary is found on the western coast of South America (see fig 58 and map). Here one plate disappears under another one. The lower plate breaks up and melts, causing earthquakes and volcanoes. The upper crumples to form fold mountains. In the ocean there is a deep **ocean trench** where one plate goes under the other.

Activity B

1 Add to your dictionary the words in bold type.

2 Find an atlas showing the different depths in the ocean. Find the mid-ocean ridge in the Atlantic Ocean, and the deep ocean trench on the western coast of South America. How deep is the water? Name some islands on the mid-ocean ridge.

3 The movement of plates means the Atlantic Ocean is getting larger and the Pacific Ocean is getting smaller. Try to explain in 3 or 4 sentences why you think this is happening.

4 If the land has been moving for millions of years, the land will have been in different positions in the past. A map of the world would have looked very different then. Try cutting up a world map of continents and re-arranging the parts to see what possible patterns there might have been. The arrows on the world map should help you.

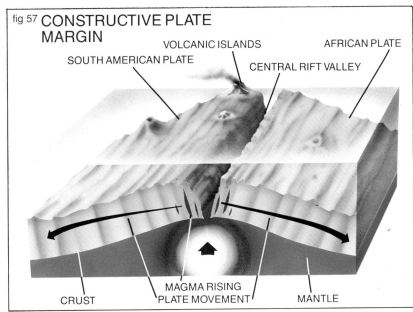

fig 57 **CONSTRUCTIVE PLATE MARGIN**

VOLCANIC ISLANDS

SOUTH AMERICAN PLATE

AFRICAN PLATE

CENTRAL RIFT VALLEY

CRUST

MAGMA RISING
PLATE MOVEMENT

MANTLE

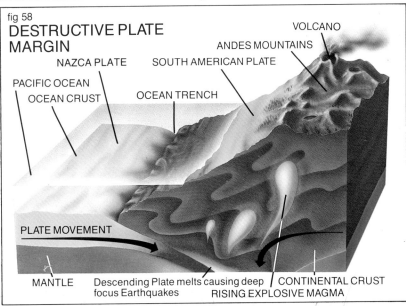

fig 58
DESTRUCTIVE PLATE MARGIN

VOLCANO

ANDES MOUNTAINS

NAZCA PLATE

SOUTH AMERICAN PLATE

PACIFIC OCEAN
OCEAN CRUST

OCEAN TRENCH

PLATE MOVEMENT

MANTLE

Descending Plate melts causing deep focus Earthquakes

CONTINENTAL CRUST
RISING EXPLOSIVE MAGMA

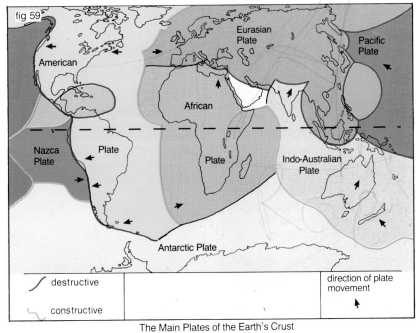

fig 59

Eurasian Plate

Pacific Plate

American

African

Plate

Nazca Plate

Plate

Plate

Indo-Australian Plate

Antarctic Plate

destructive

constructive

direction of plate movement

The Main Plates of the Earth's Crust

The Active Crust

The features of plates and their edges can be seen by looking at one ocean in detail. The cross-section of the Atlantic Ocean shows that it has as much variety of scenery as the land. This is a constructive plate boundary, here you can find:

- **the mid-Atlantic ridge** a chain of mountains on the centre of the ocean floor
- **volcanic islands** the peaks of some of these mountains
- **ocean plains** stretching from the mid-atlantic ridge to the continental shelf
- **older extinct volcanoes** on the ocean plains
- **ocean deeps** sometimes in the form of deep trenches on the edges of the oceans
- **continental shelves** marking the true edge of the continents

A small part of the Pacific Ocean and the west coast of South America is shown to contrast with the mid-Atlantic ridge. This is a destructive plate boundary, here there are:

- **the Andes mountains**, continental young fold mountains parallel to the coast
- **explosive volcanoes** on the edge of the continent
- **deep ocean trench** off the coast
- **ocean plains** of the Pacific

Activity A

1 Look at fig 60, and use an atlas to name:

a the lines you would find at 1 to 5 (latitudes)

b continents 6 to 10

c islands 11 to 14

2 Look at the coastlines south of the Tropic of Cancer. What do you notice about their shapes? Do they 'fit' together?

3 What does this suggest about previous positions of South America and Africa?

4 Where in the Atlantic Ocean will new crust be made?

5 What suggests that the sea floor is spreading out from the mid-Atlantic ridge?

6 Draw a copy of the section, and add the direction of plate movement.

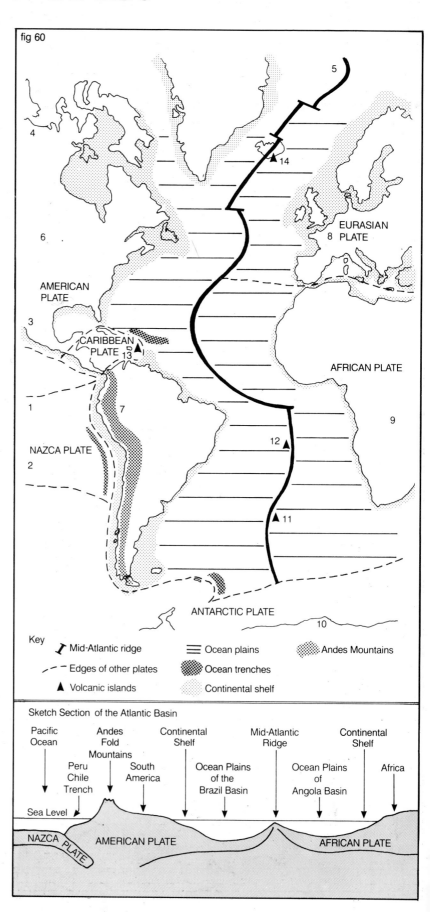

fig 60

EURASIAN PLATE

AMERICAN PLATE

CARIBBEAN PLATE

AFRICAN PLATE

NAZCA PLATE

ANTARCTIC PLATE

Key

⌐ Mid-Atlantic ridge

– – Edges of other plates

▲ Volcanic islands

≡ Ocean plains

▓ Ocean trenches

▒ Continental shelf

░ Andes Mountains

Sketch Section of the Atlantic Basin

Pacific Ocean | Andes Fold Mountains | Continental Shelf | Mid-Atlantic Ridge | Continental Shelf

Peru Chile Trench | South America | Ocean Plains of the Brazil Basin | Ocean Plains of Angola Basin | Africa

Sea Level

NAZCA PLATE | AMERICAN PLATE | AFRICAN PLATE

The plates of the earth's crust move about carrying the continents with them. The continents were therefore in different positions in the past, and today they are still moving:

- South America is moving away from Africa
- North America and Europe are getting further apart
- India is moving north into Asia and this continues to raise the Himalayan fold mountains

The slow movement over millions of years is known as **continental drift**. The evidence of a continent's former positions is found in the record of its rocks. Coal forms in tropical forest swamps, but it is found today in the rocks under the ice sheets of Antarctica. In the Kalahari Desert of South West Africa, there are rocks that form only under ice sheets. Africa and Antarctica therefore must have had different positions in the past.

These rocks are found in Britain:

- **Old Red Sandstone** in Devon and Cornwall formed in deserts of nearly 400 million years ago
- **mountain limestones** found in Derbyshire and the Pennines, formed from corals in the warm, tropical shallow seas of the Carboniferous period about 320 million years ago
- **coal seams** in northern Britain formed about 280 million years ago in the tropical forest swamps of the time
- **New Red Sandstone** of north-west England; from a second desert period of about 220 million years ago

Britain must have moved northward through several different environments to its present position. The rocks would then have formed in these environments:

- desert like the Kalahari region now
- warm tropical seas like those just off the coast in the Tropics, south of the Equator
- equatorial forests, similar to those of the Amazon or Zaire Lowland Basins
- desert, north of the Equator, like the Sahara

The continental drift must have been slow because otherwise the record of this passage could not have been preserved.

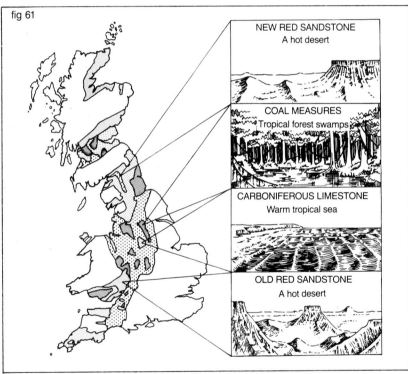

fig 61

NEW RED SANDSTONE
A hot desert

COAL MEASURES
Tropical forest swamps

CARBONIFEROUS LIMESTONE
Warm tropical sea

OLD RED SANDSTONE
A hot desert

Activity B

1 What is continental drift?
2 Write down three examples of this movement.
3 List the four rocks of Britain shown in fig 61, in order of age.
4 Name two rocks formed in dry conditions.
5 Where in Britain are Carboniferous limestones found?
6 How old are the coal rocks of Britain?
7 In not less than 100 words, write your own description of the changes in Britain's position during the period of 400 million to 220 million years ago.
8 Add to your dictionary the following: ocean plains, continental shelf, continental drift, and Carboniferous.

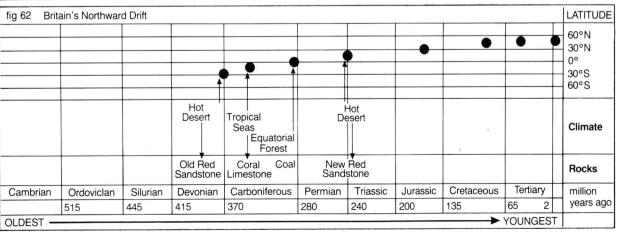

fig 62   Britain's Northward Drift

											LATITUDE
								●	●	●	60°N
						●	●				30°N
				●	●						0°
			●								30°S
											60°S
			Hot Desert	Tropical Seas / Equatorial Forest		Hot Desert					**Climate**
			Old Red Sandstone	Coral Limestone Coal		New Red Sandstone					**Rocks**
Cambrian	Ordoviclan	Silurian	Devonian	Carboniferous	Permian	Triassic	Jurassic	Cretaceous	Tertiary		million years ago
	515	445	415	370	280	240	200	135	65 2		

OLDEST ————————————————————————→ YOUNGEST

Types of Rocks

The earth's crustal plates are made of many different kinds of rocks. Rock type depends on:
- the original material from which it was made
- how it was formed
- how it has been altered since then

The four examples of rocks in Britain studied on page 45 are all similar, they were all formed from fragments or particles which were laid down or deposited in layers and converted into rock. Such deposited fragments are called sediments and so this type of rock is known as **sedimentary**. They can be made of:
- broken particles of other rocks
- plant and animal remains
- chemicals left after evaporation of water

The layers in which the sediments are deposited are known as beds. A change from one layer to the next, often a line of weakness, is called a **bedding plane**.

1 Rocks from Sediments

Activity A
1 Answer these questions in sentences:
a what are the earth's crustal plates made of?
b what determines rock type?
c what is a sediment?
d name three sediments that form rocks.
e name four sedimentary rocks that are formed from the broken particles of other rocks.
f name one example of rock formed from animal remains.

2 *The desert sandstone is orangey-brown in colour. The surface of the rock looks and feels gritty as the grains are of medium size. Under the hand lens these grains are seen to be polished and rounded. The grains are separated from one another by tiny air spaces. The specimen contains no fossils. It does not react with weak acids.*

Describe other rocks of your choice, using this example for ideas. Make sure you mention at least five facts.
3 Add sedimentary rock to your dictionary.

fig 63
Environments of Sediments

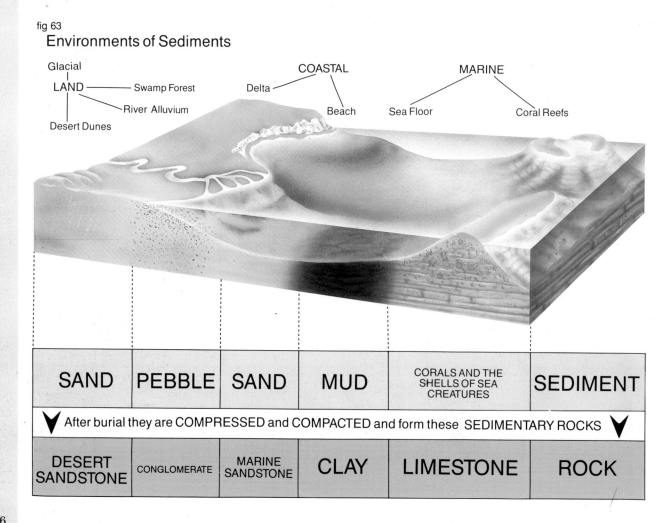

SAND	PEBBLE	SAND	MUD	CORALS AND THE SHELLS OF SEA CREATURES	SEDIMENT

▼ After burial they are COMPRESSED and COMPACTED and form these SEDIMENTARY ROCKS ▼

DESERT SANDSTONE	CONGLOMERATE	MARINE SANDSTONE	CLAY	LIMESTONE	ROCK

2 Rocks from Magma

Some rocks are formed when molten lava cools and hardens. The minerals in the lava form interlocking crystals when they cool. Volcanic lava normally contains very small crystals since they do not have time to grow when the lava can cool quickly, such as in air or on the sea bed. If the lava cannot reach the surface it cools much more slowly, so that there is time for the crystals to grow. This type of rock therefore has larger crystals.

Crystalline rocks made by the cooling of molten lava or magma are called **igneous** rocks. Two common igneous rocks are **basalt** and **granite**.

When lava from volcanoes like Mauna Loa cools it forms a very dark coloured rock with fine crystals (see page 36). This is basalt (shown in photo 32). The scenery is typical of lava that cooled very quickly and contracted, seen in photo 33. This has caused cracks in the rocks. These cracks are called **joints** and in basalt they often form six-sided columns.

Photos 34 and 35 show a different rock. The crystals in this rock are very much larger. There are three kinds of crystal:
- clear, shining crystals of **quartz**
- white and pinkish **felspar**
- black shiny **mica**

The rock formed from these three minerals is called granite. This rock was formed by cooling at depth in the earth's crust, its crystals are therefore much larger. It is found on the surface millions of years later after covering rocks have been worn away.

Activity B

1 Name two common igneous rocks.
2 Which one is found in volcanoes?
3 Where does the other one form?
4 Write out the following, filling in the missing words:
Rocks which form from molten lava or magma are called . . . . rocks. When the lava cools slowly, the . . . . in the rock grow large, but when it cools . . . ., they are much . . . .
5 Add igneous rock to your dictionary.
6 Write sentences describing five features of each of the two igneous rocks. Use the photographs to help.
7 Find out the names and details of other igneous rocks.
8 Find out what The Giant's Causeway, Isle of Staffa, a giant called Fingal and a composer called Mendelssohn, have to do with basalt.
9 Why is granite being quarried? Can you name four uses that granite is put to?

photo 32: Basalt rock

photo 33: Basalt scenery

photo 34: Granite rock

photo 35: Granite scenery

3 Rocks from Alterations

A third group of rocks contains **metamorphic** rocks, which have been altered or changed from their original form. The amount of energy is so large that it can only come from great heat or pressure such as that caused by the movement of the earth's plates:

- rocks can be cooked or baked when in contact with hot magma or lava
- rocks can be squeezed so that their minerals line themselves up in closely packed thin sheets
- rocks can be altered so much by both heat and pressure that it can be difficult to recognise the original rock. These are treated as completely new crystalline rock

Marble reacts with weak acid in the same way as **limestone** because the rocks are made of the same substance. The shelly fragments that make up the limestone have been crystallised by heat to form the new rock, marble.

Sideways pressure compresses thin grains of **clay** and re-arranges them to form **slate**. This rock can split along the lines of weakness into thin sheets or slabs. **Gneiss** and **schist** are crystalline rocks which have been formed by a mixture of great heat and pressure in regions of mountain building. They are so highly altered by the great heat and pressure that it is difficult to recognise the original rock. Rocks like these often contain new and unusual minerals such as **garnets**.

Activity A

1 Complete this table by using the photographs:

Original Rock Type	Process	New Rock
	Heat	Marble
Shale		
Difficult to tell	Great heat and pressure	

2 Continue adding words to your geographical dictionary.

3 Describe marble, slate, and schist rocks giving at least five facts about each in sentences.

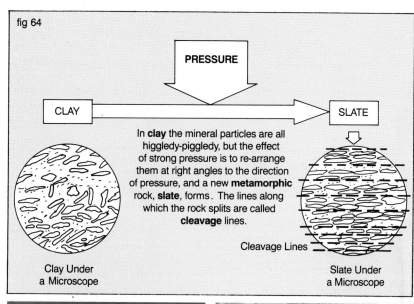

fig 64

PRESSURE

CLAY → SLATE

In **clay** the mineral particles are all higgledy-piggledy, but the effect of strong pressure is to re-arrange them at right angles to the direction of pressure, and a new **metamorphic** rock, **slate**, forms. The lines along which the rock splits are called **cleavage** lines.

Cleavage Lines

Clay Under a Microscope

Slate Under a Microscope

photo 36: Clay rock sample

photo 37: Slate rock sample

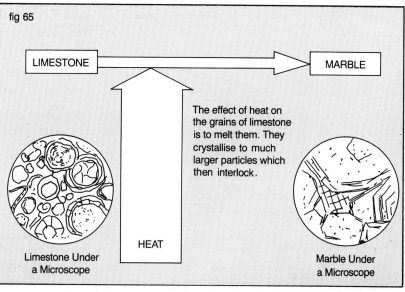

fig 65

LIMESTONE → MARBLE

The effect of heat on the grains of limestone is to melt them. They crystallise to much larger particles which then interlock.

HEAT

Limestone Under a Microscope

Marble Under a Microscope

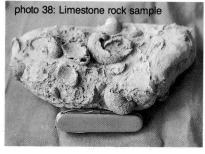

photo 38: Limestone rock sample

photo 39: Marble rock sample

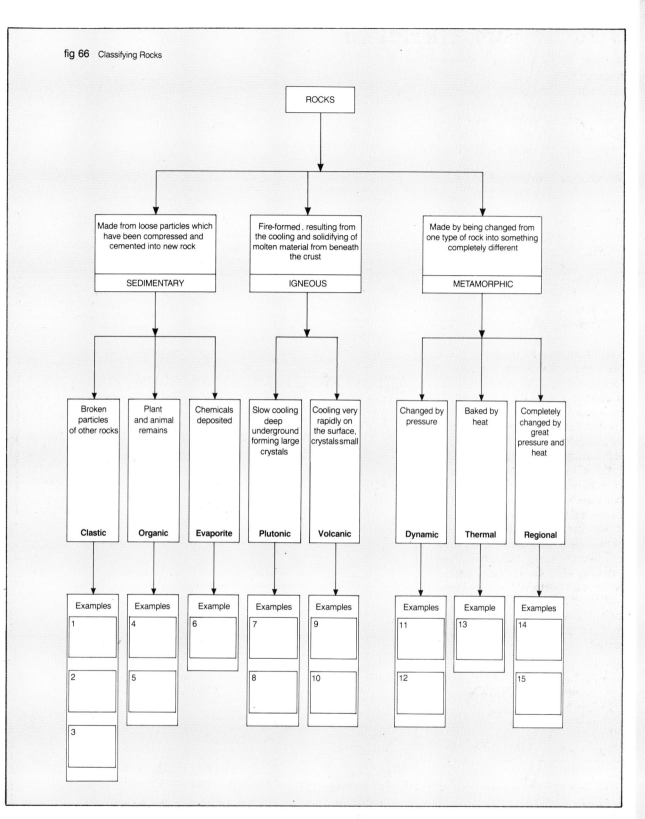

fig 66 Classifying Rocks

ROCKS

Made from loose particles which have been compressed and cemented into new rock	Fire-formed, resulting from the cooling and solidifying of molten material from beneath the crust	Made by being changed from one type of rock into something completely different
SEDIMENTARY	IGNEOUS	METAMORPHIC

SEDIMENTARY:
- Broken particles of other rocks — **Clastic**
- Plant and animal remains — **Organic**
- Chemicals deposited — **Evaporite**

IGNEOUS:
- Slow cooling deep underground forming large crystals — **Plutonic**
- Cooling very rapidly on the surface, crystals small — **Volcanic**

METAMORPHIC:
- Changed by pressure — **Dynamic**
- Baked by heat — **Thermal**
- Completely changed by great pressure and heat — **Regional**

Examples (Clastic): 1, 2, 3
Examples (Organic): 4, 5
Example (Evaporite): 6
Examples (Plutonic): 7, 8
Examples (Volcanic): 9, 10
Examples (Dynamic): 11, 12
Example (Thermal): 13
Examples (Regional): 14, 15

Activity B

1 Copy fig 66 and fill in the empty boxes with the names of the rocks you have studied. Colour in each of the main groups of rocks differently.

2 Find out about these rocks using library books: clay, chalk, dolerite, andesite and quartzite.

Write down the group each rock belongs to, how it was formed and anything unsual about them.

3 Start a rock collection. Note exactly where you found the rock, what type of rock it is, what minerals it contains and any unusual features.

Blyth Valley

Volcanoes, faults, fold mountains, plains and the rocks from which they are made are outputs of the **crustal system**. They are large-scale features created mainly by the movements of the earth's plates. The crustal system is powered by the sun's energy and by the internal energy of the earth. However, these features are only the bare bones of the scenery. The finer detail is added by the work of weather and gravity forming another set of natural processes. They wear down and re-shape the landscape. This is the **scenic system** see fig 6, page 7.

The natural processes in the scenic system are:
- **weathering** the breaking up of rocks where they lie by the direct effect of weather and plant and animal activity
- **erosion** the wearing down of the land by running water, moving ice, the wind and waves
- **transport** the carrying away of weathered and eroded material
- **deposition** the laying down of transported material in a new place

All these processes together are called **denudation**. Scenery varies so much throughout the world because these processes work differently in different situations.

This can be seen by looking at a river basin, a desert, a glaciated valley and a coastline. The river chosen for the study of a river basin is a small river in the north east of England – the River Blyth. The river with all its tributaries and the natural and artificial details of the area are shown in fig 67.

Activity A

Look at fig 67 and your atlas, to answer these questions:

1 In which county is the Blyth River found?
2 Which large river basin lies just south of that of the River Blyth?
3 What is the large city on this nearby river? How far is it from Blyth?
4 In which direction does the River Blyth flow?
5 What are the distances across the drainage basin of the River Blyth through the village of Whalton:
a from west to east?
b from north to south?
6 Name the following features found in the drainage basin of the River Blyth:
a two towns
b three villages
c one industry
7 Which main road crosses the Blyth River?
8 Which British cities does this road connect?
9 From your answers to these questions, and from information on the map, try to write a description of the geography of the River Blyth basin.
10 Continue with your geographical dictionary.

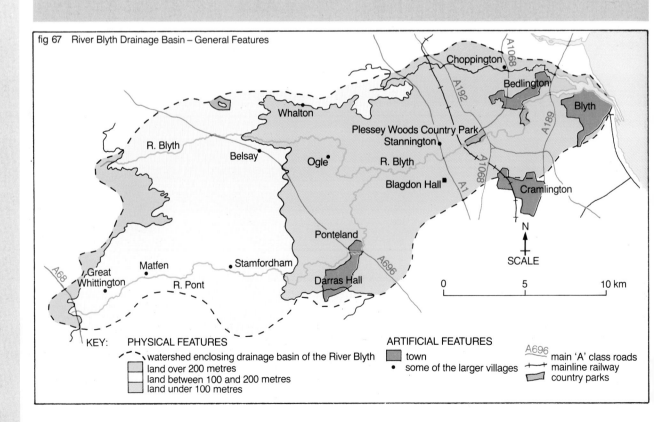

fig 67   River Blyth Drainage Basin – General Features

KEY: PHYSICAL FEATURES

- - - watershed enclosing drainage basin of the River Blyth
land over 200 metres
land between 100 and 200 metres
land under 100 metres

ARTIFICIAL FEATURES

town
• some of the larger villages

A696 main 'A' class roads
mainline railway
country parks

When precipitation falls on to the land it forms surface water or **run off**, this collects into small channels forming streams. The head of a stream is called its **source**. The stream flows downhill, and is joined by other streams or **tributaries**. The join is called a **confluence**. As more tributaries join the stream, it becomes larger and forms a river. The river widens out as it enters the sea, here it becomes an **estuary**. The place where the river joins the sea is called its **mouth**. The area of land from which all the water comes into the river is called its **drainage basin**. This is also the **catchment area** for the precipitation which will eventually flow into the river. The edge of this area is called the **watershed**. If rain falls outside this, it will join another river's system. Can you see all of these on the River Blyth?

Stream ordering is one way of describing and comparing drainage basins (see fig 68). Streams are given a number according to their size and position: the smallest streams are class 1, and when they join they become a class 2; from then on the stream only goes up a class if it meets another one of the same number. The River Blyth is a class 4 river, in an area of 321 km². It has the following individual classes:

class 1	70 streams
class 2	19 streams
class 3	6 streams
class 4	1 stream

photo 40 Confluence on the River Blyth

Activity B
1 Look carefully at fig 68
a which is the main tributary and what class is it?
b how many class 1 streams are there?
c to what feature are they near?
d on average, how many class 1 streams are there for every class 2 stream?
2 Design and draw an imaginary river basin with:
eight class 1 streams
four class 2 streams
two class 3 streams
one class 4 stream
Mark a watershed on your drawing.
3 Work out the details of a small river basin near to where you live.

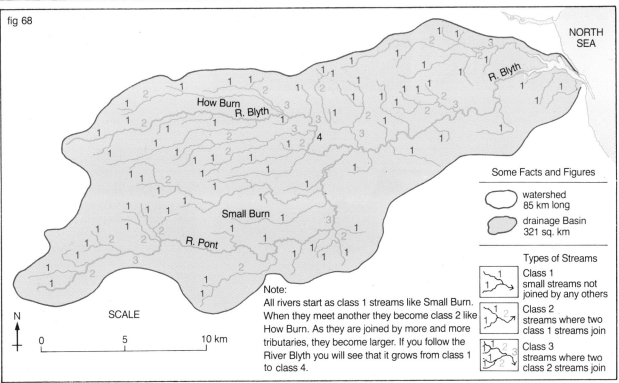
fig 68

Note:
All rivers start as class 1 streams like Small Burn. When they meet another they become class 2 like How Burn. As they are joined by more and more tributaries, they become larger. If you follow the River Blyth you will see that it grows from class 1 to class 4.

People in the Blyth Valley

photo 41

photo 42

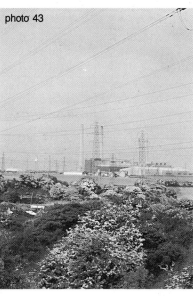

photo 43

The River Blyth and its drainage basin have been important to people who have lived in the area throughout history.

- farms and small villages are widely scattered throughout the basin, they were originally built next to streams for water supply (photo 41)
- Blyth grew up as a coal exporting port at the mouth of the river; it was also a coal mining town, and acted as the market for the local area. It now has several modern light industrial estates (photo 42)
- a power station was built on the estuary of the river, where there are very large amounts of water for cooling. It provides electricity not only for the people and industries of the Blyth Valley area but for all north east England. It is fired by coal, found in the rocks underlying the basin (photo 43) The river is also used to remove waste products. Without proper care the value of the river to people will be reduced
- Plessey Woods Country Park shows how land use can change over time. In the nineteenth century this was an area of coal mining, and stone quarrying. Now that the coal has been worked out the woodland area is a country park visited and enjoyed by the local town dwellers (photo 44)

photo 44

Activity A
1 Using fig 67 on page 50 draw a sketch map to show the following features: the coast, the watershed, the rivers Blyth and Pont, and the main towns.
2 Blyth is an area of high unemployment. Design a four-page booklet showing the attractions of the area to people wishing to set up factories and live there with their families.

River Scenery

photo 45

fig 69

dolerite
more resistant rock
walls of gorge
limestone
less resistant rock
plunge pool
river Tees

photo 46

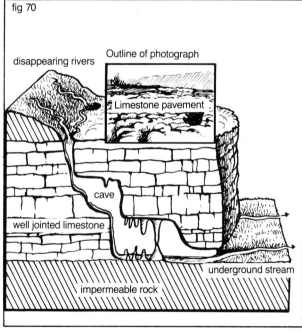

fig 70

disappearing rivers
Outline of photograph
Limestone pavement
cave
well jointed limestone
underground stream
impermeable rock

No two river basins have the same scenery. While all rivers work in the same way, the results can depend on the different rocks they flow over.

- the hard igneous rock of High Force in Upper Teesdale is more resistant than the underlying limestone. The River Tees has been unable to wear it down as fast and so a large waterfall results (photo 45)
- the high limestone hillsides of the Pennines resist river erosion.

There are few surface rivers or streams because the rainwater sinks through cracks or joints in the rock. The rock is therefore resistant to river erosion as it is **permeable** or lets water pass through it. Many features of limestone scenery occur underground (photo 46)

River processes produce widely varying landforms and scenery as they work in many different structures of land produced by

the crustal system such as

- volcanoes, faults and folds
- combinations of rock types
- weather or climatic regions
- lengths of geological time

Activity B
Look at the two photographs of a waterfall and of a limestone pavement. For each one, describe the appearance of the scenery.

Down the valley . . .

Here are three photographs of different parts of the Blyth and Pont rivers. Photo 47 shows the upper reaches of the River Pont near its source. Here it is a small, narrow class 1 stream.

Photo 48 is further down the valley where many more tributaries have joined the main river. It shows the River Blyth just below its confluence with the River Pont. At this point it has become a class 3 river with a much wider, flatter valley.

The features near the mouth of the River Blyth where it is a class 4 river are shown in photo 49. At this place the river winds its way through a nearly flat landscape. Much of this is made of **alluvium** – the fine material transported by the river and deposited here.

The **long profile** of a river is a graph showing how its height changes from source to mouth. Fig 71 shows the longest profile of the Blyth valley. This goes from the class 1 beginning of the River Pont through to the mouth of the class 4 River Blyth.

photo 47: Upper valley

photo 48: Middle valley

photo 49: Lower valley

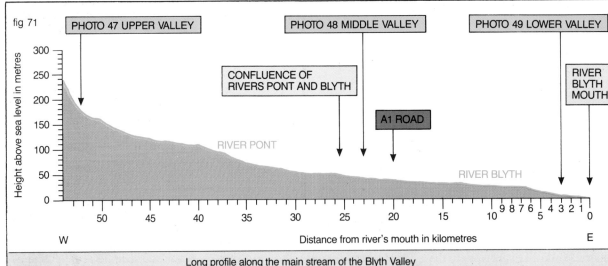

Long profile along the main stream of the Blyth Valley

Activity A

1 Look at photo 47 and then answer these questions:
a approximately how wide is the stream?
b what shape is the valley it flows in?
c what class will the stream be here?
d describe the load of the stream.
e what do you notice about the banks of the stream?
f how straight is the valley?
g suggest why this is sometimes described as **interlocking spurs**.

2 Write a description of the other two photos in the same way.

3 Add these to your dictionary: long profile; alluvium; interlocking spurs.

4 Describe the changes you would see along a river valley on a journey from source to mouth.

. . . the River is Working

Sediment is broken or weathered rock particles from the valley sides and the material worn away by the river from its bed and banks. The transport of this load is done in four ways:

- **traction** by rolling stones along the bed
- **saltation** by particles bouncing in a jumping movement over the river bed
- **suspension** by smaller particles being carried entirely in the water flow
- **solution** by the load dissolving in the water

Any particle may move in more than one of these ways, it depends on the changes in the energy of the stream or river. At times of flood, the river will carry a greater load. The heaviest boulders and stones may only be moved in floods, by rolling or traction.

As well as transporting its load, a river will also wear away the rocks over which it passes. This erosion takes place in four ways:

- **hydraulic action** the force of flowing water, which is sometimes enough to dislodge particles from the bed and banks of the river
- **corrasion** particles in the water hit the bed and banks and help to wear them away

photo 50: Erosion by the river
Erosion

- **attrition** particles in the water knock against each other and the sides of the bank, they therefore get smaller and more rounded as they move downstream
- **corrosion** rocks and minerals can be dissolved chemically in the water

These four processes can go on all the time. Dramatic work can be done when the river's energy is suddenly and rapidly increased as in floods.

Deposition happens throughout a river's course. It is the laying down of part of the load when the river does not have enough energy to transport it. This is common in the upper reaches of a river. It is usually only in times of high water or flood that a lot of this coarse material can be moved. By contrast, lower down the river the load is much finer and is deposited where the river currents are slow, this will happen in shallow places where energy is lost in overcoming friction. Deposition is common on the inside of the river bends or meanders.

photo 51: Deposition by the river
Deposition

Activity B

1 What is the name of the sediment carried by a river?
2 Where does this sediment come from?
3 Describe 4 ways of transporting this sediement.
4 Explain how a river erodes.
5 What is deposition?
6 Why does it happen?
7 In not less than 100 words, describe what will happen to work done by a river during a flood. Use headings of energy, transport, erosion and deposition.

How to Measure a River

The work of a river is a combination of transport, erosion and deposition. To find out what a stream is doing at any time requires accurate observation and measurement:

- **depth** is measured by using a survey pole. A line is stretched from one bank to another and depths measured across this at regular intervals. Halving the width of a river can sometimes give an idea of the depth
- **width** can be measured by getting your feet wet and measuring from A to B on the diagram. Or you can trace out the triangle CAB on to your bank, as CDE, since the distance DE will be the same as AB
- **speed or velocity** is measured by throwing a bright object (such as an orange) in the water at position D on the diagram. The recorder writes down the time the object takes to float between the person at C and at B (the object should be floating at the speed of the river by now). The object is thrown in several times at X, Y and Z, and then an average is taken of the recordings. This is then divided by 5 to give the speed in metres per second
- **discharge** is calculated from the formula discharge (m³/sec) = width (m) × depth (m) × speed (m/sec)

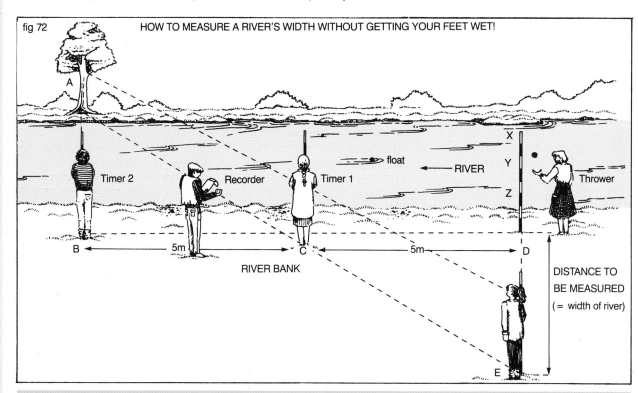

fig 72   HOW TO MEASURE A RIVER'S WIDTH WITHOUT GETTING YOUR FEET WET!

Timer 2 · Recorder · Timer 1 · float · RIVER · Thrower · X · Y · Z

B — 5m — C — 5m — D

RIVER BANK

DISTANCE TO BE MEASURED (= width of river)

E

Activity A

1 These are some measurements taken from the River Blyth near Plessey woods on an August afternoon.

Width of River 17 metres		
Time taken to travel 5 metres (in seconds)		
Left Bank (X)	Middle of Stream (Y)	Right Bank (Z)
10	8	9
14	9	10
12	7	10
10	7	12
13	8	10
13	7	11
12	9	12
10	8	10

Work out: **a** the average time taken to travel 5 metres at X, Y, Z

b the average speeds at X, Y and Z

c overall average speed of the river

d average depth (assuming that width is twice depth)

2 Copy out the formula for river discharge. Use the figures from the River Blyth to work out the discharge on that August afternoon. The discharge is unusually low since the measurements were taken in the middle of the 1984 drought.

3 Add to your dictionary the words velocity, discharge and energy.

4 Explain how the width and speed of a river can be measured.

5 Measure local streams in the same drainage basin, of different stream order classes. Then measure streams of the same classes at different times. What conclusions can you come to?

THE WORK OF A RIVER

fig 73

| SILT and CLAY | not enough energy to move silt and clay **Deposition** | just enough energy to move silt and clay **Transport** | | more energy than required to move silt and clay **Erosion** | |
| PEBBLES and BOULDERS | | | | | |

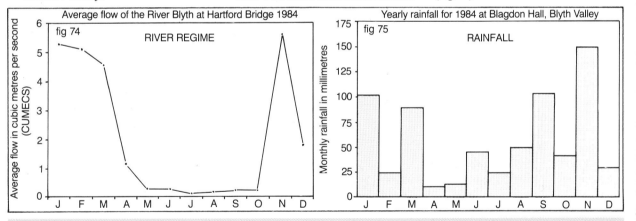

SAND	not enough energy to move sand **Deposition**		just enough energy to move sand **Transport**	more energy than required to move sand **Erosion**	
PEBBLES and BOULDERS	not enough energy to move pebbles and boulders **Deposition** 1			just enough to move **Transport** 2	more energy than required to move **Erosion** 3

speed of river ⟶ FAST

The following grouping of streams can be made in some areas:

- **smaller lower order streams** of class 1 or 2 are narrow and shallow but the discharge changes greatly between wet and dry weather. They often seem fast flowing, but usually have a small volume and little energy. They lose much of their energy due to friction with the irregular and stony bed. It is only in occasional floods that they transport the coarse load and erode steep narrow valleys

- **middle order streams** of class 2 or 3 have a greater volume, width and depth with more energy to transport and erode. Floodwater greatly increases their effectiveness. They erode much wider broader valleys

- **high order streams** of class 4 and over have the greatest volume. Their flow varies from time to time, but much less so than with smaller streams. They use a lot of their energy in transport and erode more sideways into their banks than downwards into the bed. The most noticeable feature

is the amount of deposition; this helps make the very wide, shallow valley shape and the formation of flood plains. The load becomes finer downstream and is deposited in parts of the channel where there is slower flowing water

The flow of a river is constantly changing from day to day. But from year to year the pattern is much more regular. The **regime** or yearly pattern of discharge for the River Blyth (fig 74) can be compared against the monthly rainfall figures (fig 75).

Average flow of the River Blyth at Hartford Bridge 1984

fig 74 — RIVER REGIME

(Average flow in cubic metres per second (CUMECS) plotted J–D)

Yearly rainfall for 1984 at Blagdon Hall, Blyth Valley

fig 75 — RAINFALL

(Monthly rainfall in millimetres plotted J–D)

Activity B

1 On one sheet of graph paper:

a copy the regime graph (fig 74) on the top half.

b underneath it, draw a bar graph to show the yearly pattern of rainfall. Be careful to match up the months on both graphs.

2 Write down the months, and their figures, which have the highest discharge; the highest rainfall; the lowest discharge; and the lowest rainfall.

3 Compare the two graphs and describe any similarities in the patterns of river discharge and rainfall.

4 Copy fig 73, showing the size of the load in a river

and the speed of the water needed to transport and erode it. Colour in red where deposition occurs, yellow where transport occurs and green where erosion occurs. Then answer these questions:

a what happens to a boulder at the speeds of the river marked 1, 2 and 3?

b what happens to a pebble as the speed of the river changes from slow to fast?

c what work will be done by sand particles when the river flows fast?

d how does this change as the speed of the river gets less?

Patterns of Scenery

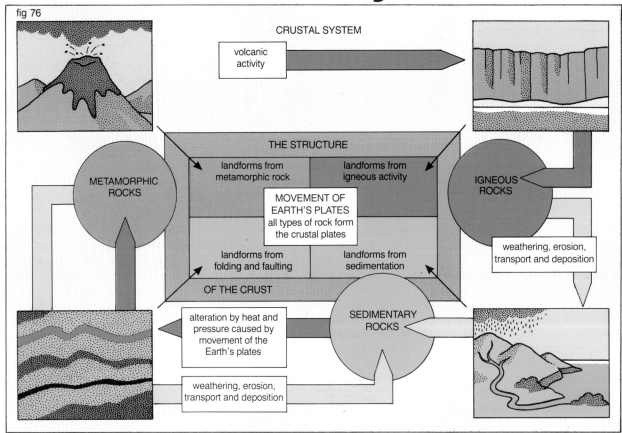

fig 76

CRUSTAL SYSTEM

volcanic activity

THE STRUCTURE

METAMORPHIC ROCKS

landforms from metamorphic rock

landforms from igneous activity

MOVEMENT OF EARTH'S PLATES
all types of rock form the crustal plates

IGNEOUS ROCKS

landforms from folding and faulting

landforms from sedimentation

weathering, erosion, transport and deposition

OF THE CRUST

alteration by heat and pressure caused by movement of the Earth's plates

SEDIMENTARY ROCKS

weathering, erosion, transport and deposition

A system has inputs, component parts linked by flows of energy and materials and an output. The Blyth valley scenic system has:
- **input** in the form of rain, snow and other forms of precipitation
- a pattern of sedimentary rocks, streams and valley slopes as its **component** parts
- the flow of the streams provide the **energy**
- the scenery and landforms as its **output**

This is really only one small part of system earth, and is linked with many other systems. The weather system provides one input in the form of precipitation. The crustal system provides the pattern of rocks and their arrangement which the river system has worked.
In turn, sediments taken to the sea by the river makes an input back into the crustal system. These sediments will eventually become the new sedimentary rocks of the future.

These pages revise the crustal and scenic systems and some of the links between them.
One way of showing the crustal system is fig 76. It displays both the features of the crust and its rocks as well as the processes operating on them. Most of the processes result from movements of the earth's crustal plates and are part of the crustal system. These are shown in red, but those shown in blue are also part of the scenic system.

Activity A

1 Copy out the passage choosing the correct alternatives.

New material from the $\frac{core}{mantle}$ reaches the surface as $\frac{volcanoes}{epicentres}$ which erupt it in the form of $\frac{alluvium}{lava}$. When it cools down it forms $\frac{igneous}{sedimentary}$ rock. This rock will be attacked by the agents of $\frac{metamorphism}{denudation}$ and broken into small fragments. These particles will be $\frac{deposited}{condensed}$ and will eventually form new $\frac{igneous}{sedimentary}$ rock. If the plates of the earth's $\frac{crust}{core}$ move then these new rocks can be $\frac{folded}{precipitated}$ into mountains. Heat and pressure of this can change the rocks into new $\frac{sedimentary}{metamorphic}$ rocks. All these processes are part of $\frac{crustal}{system}$ earth.

2 Collect colour pictures of volcanoes, rocks, minerals, fossils, mountains, valleys and other items or features of the earth's crust. These can be found in Sunday newspapers, colour supplements, magazines and tourist brochures.

3 Make a wall poster of fig 76. Stick your pictures on it in suitable positions to illustrate it.

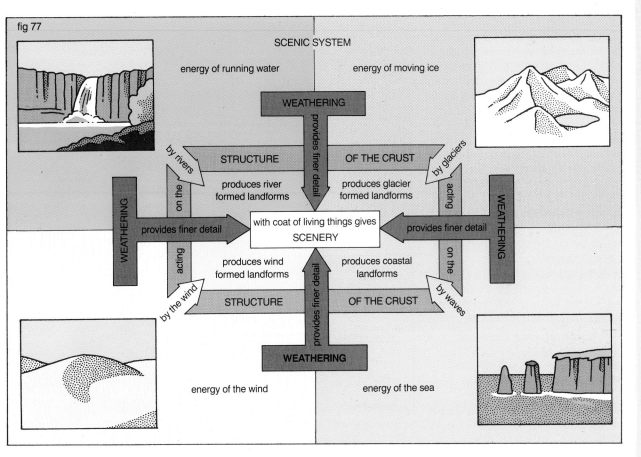

fig 77

SCENIC SYSTEM

energy of running water   energy of moving ice

WEATHERING

STRUCTURE   OF THE CRUST

produces river formed landforms   produces glacier formed landforms

WEATHERING — provides finer detail

with coat of living things gives SCENERY

provides finer detail — WEATHERING

produces wind formed landforms   produces coastal landforms

STRUCTURE   OF THE CRUST

WEATHERING

energy of the wind   energy of the sea

Rivers and running water are one example of a moving agent of denudation. Moving ice, the wind and waves are the others. Weathering is also a denudational agent, but it acts without movement in the breaking down of rocks.

Together, all these five agents produce scenery through the processes of transport, erosion and deposition. They obtain their power from the sun via the atmospheric system. This power is converted into available energy for work when they move over the structures and features of mountains, slopes and plains of the earth's crustal plates.

These agents work within the scenic system to shape the scenery (fig 77). Each moving agent operates in the system in the following ways:
- it obtains its energy mostly through the atmospheric system
- it moves over regions of the crustal system
- it transports, erodes and deposits broken rock fragments

Activity B
1 Draw the full diagram of the scenic system.
2 What is denudation?
3 Name one static and four moving agents of denudation.
4 Write out in your own words the four stages by which moving agents help create patterns of scenery.
5 There are twenty words in this puzzle. Find them, and write out their meanings without looking in your dictionary of geography. The words are written horizontally or vertically only, and letters can be used in more than one word.

The remaining letters spell out a message. Write it out.

6 Revise the words in your dictionary ready for a test on their meanings.

```
P C O E N A C I R R U H N M
R G R P E L O N G I T U D E
E N V I R O N M E N T A T T
C U O C O L A T I O Y I N A
I S L E S A S E N E R G Y M
P Y C N I O U L H G E N A O
I A A T O P V B E R N E L R
T A N R N L S A O A E O L P
A V O E L A V E E H C U U H
T A S Y S T E M D C S S V I
I L O A D E T R H S I S I C
O R O T A U Q E P I U Z U Z
N O I T I S O P E D L E M !
```

The Great American Desert

These **coastal dunes** are formed when wind blows across the wide sandy beach. It helps to dry the sand at low tide. The finer particles of sand are then picked up by the wind and blow inland. The sand collects and as more and more sand is deposited a dune is formed. The climate is wet enough to encourage plants like marram grass to grow on the dry salty sands. This grass binds the sand together with its root system and helps to prevent the dune from moving.

Photo 53 shows an area called the Great American Desert.

A desert is a region in which there is not enough rainfall for permanent settlement. Most of the world's **hot deserts** are shown in the map.

These **desert sand dunes**

- cover a wide area
- are crescent shaped in plan
- have one steep side and one gently sloping side
- have ripple marks on their surface
- have very few plants growing on them, so the loose sand is moved easily by the wind

The coastal dunes of the Blyth Valley and the desert dunes of Death Valley in the south west USA both result from the action of the wind. The scenery of each place is very different because other processes affecting the landscape in each region are not the same.

photo 52: Blyth valley

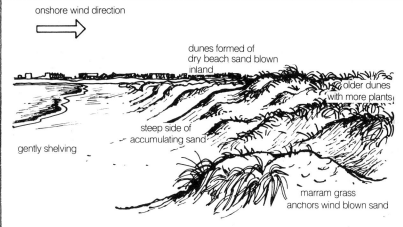

onshore wind direction

dunes formed of dry beach sand blown inland

older dunes with more plants

steep side of accumulating sand

gently shelving

marram grass anchors wind blown sand

A special type of desert sand dune is a **barchan** dune. This is formed when wind blows largely from one direction across a wide desert plain. The wind picks up the finer sand particles. The sand which is moved will collect against obstacles such as stones. Sand deposits build up. As there is less sand around the edges these will move forward faster and form the wings of the dune and give it the characteristic shape – a crescent.

photo 53: Death valley sand dunes, U.S.A.

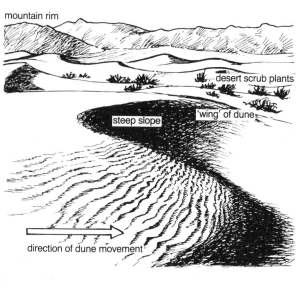

mountain rim

desert scrub plants

steep slope

'wing' of dune

direction of dune movement

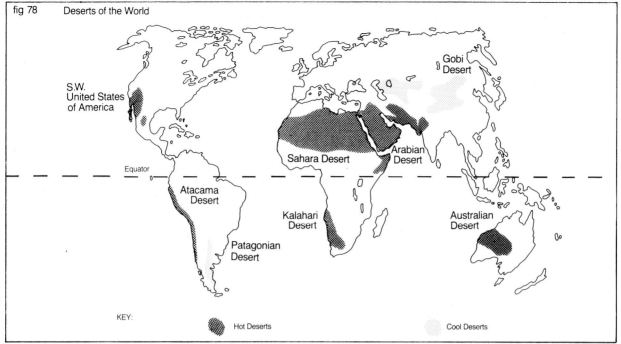

fig 78   Deserts of the World

Gobi Desert

S.W. United States of America

Sahara Desert

Arabian Desert

Equator

Atacama Desert

Kalahari Desert

Australian Desert

Patagonian Desert

KEY: ⬤ Hot Deserts   ▒ Cool Deserts

Every landscape is the result of the work of the crustal system altered by the work of the agents of denudation. The special character of any region depends on a combination of processes. These may act together or at different times.

● the scenery of Blyth Valley is the result of rain water on rocks that are nearly horizontal. Along the coast processes of **waves** and **wind** are at work forming the landscape

● in the south-west USA the process forming dunes operates in a dry or **arid** climate. Running water does not greatly affect this scenery today although it was quite effective in the past when there was a wetter climate

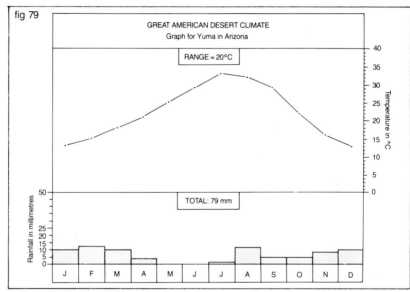

fig 79

GREAT AMERICAN DESERT CLIMATE
Graph for Yuma in Arizona

RANGE = 20°C

Temperature in °C

TOTAL: 79 mm

Rainfall in millimetres

J F M A M J J A S O N D

Activity

1 Copy this table into your book and use the information on this page together with the diagrams and photographs to compare the two types of dunes.

	Coastal Dunes	Desert Dunes
Where found		
Size		
Shape		
How formed		
Surface Appearance		

2 Look at the map of the hot deserts of the world, fig 78.

a on an outline map of the world shade in the areas of hot deserts.

b mark on your outline map the Equator and the Tropics of Cancer and Capricorn. Name them.

c use your atlas to find the names of the Hot Deserts of the World and add the names to your map.

d draw a table showing the country and continent of these deserts.

3 Find the climate figures for a different hot desert. Draw a climate graph using these figures. Describe any similarities and differences between your graph and fig 79.

4 Use your school library to find out about other kinds of desert scenery; try these words first: Regir, Hamada, Zeugen, Yardang, and Wadi. Are all deserts sandy?

A Look at the Desert

The deserts of the south western part of the USA, in the State of California, Nevada and Arizona, are show in fig 80. The green line on the map joins all places with a yearly rainfall of only 250 mm. Any such line joining places with equal rainfall is called an **isohyet**. This isohyet marks the approximate edge of the deserts in this region.

This dry region is made up of several differently named desert areas such as Death Valley, the Painted Desert, the Mojave Desert and the Sonoran Desert. It also contains the Grand Canyon which has been deeply eroded by the Colorado River which passes through the region.

The cross-section drawing helps explain the pattern of the different desert areas. It shows ranges of uplifted mountain blocks and low desert basins in between, found in Death Valley, this is called **basin and range** scenery. Sand dunes are found in some parts of the basins but are only one type of feature found there.

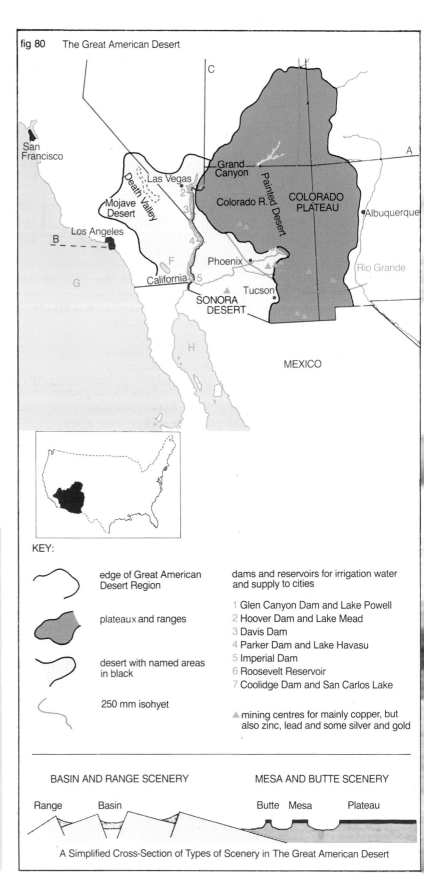

fig 80   The Great American Desert

KEY:

edge of Great American Desert Region

plateaux and ranges

desert with named areas in black

250 mm isohyet

dams and reservoirs for irrigation water and supply to cities

1 Glen Canyon Dam and Lake Powell
2 Hoover Dam and Lake Mead
3 Davis Dam
4 Parker Dam and Lake Havasu
5 Imperial Dam
6 Roosevelt Reservoir
7 Coolidge Dam and San Carlos Lake

▲ mining centres for mainly copper, but also zinc, lead and some silver and gold

BASIN AND RANGE SCENERY

Range   Basin

MESA AND BUTTE SCENERY

Butte Mesa   Plateau

A Simplified Cross-Section of Types of Scenery in The Great American Desert

Activity A

1 Look at fig 80 of the south-west United States of America. Use your atlas to answer these questions:

a give the latitude of lines A and B and the longitude of line C.

b name the two main tributaries of the Colorado River, marked D and E on the map.

c what is the name of the inland sea labelled F?

d name the two ocean areas G and H.

e draw an accurate copy of the map with all these places marked.

2 Why is this scenery called basin and range?

3 What is an isohyet?

4 Add any new words to your dictionary.

photo 54: The Grand Canyon

photo 55: Irrigating a citrus orchard

photo 56: Mining copper

photo 57: Las Vegas

photo 58: Chapparal vegetation

The lack of rainfall means that only a few people can live in this desert region, they live in:

- irrigated areas near wells along the river plains
- mining areas where there are valuable minerals
- towns and cities
- on isolated ranches in the dry scrubland or **chapparal**

All these activities need the development of water supplies.

Activity B

1 Name three dams on the map.
2 List the minerals on the map.
3 Which of the following describe the minerals you have listed:
fuels; building materials; non-ferrous metal ores; ferrous metal ores; precious metals.
4 Why is irrigation so important to this region?
5 Imagine you are a travel agent. You plan a two-week holiday package in this region for English visitors. This holiday must start at Las Vegas and finish at Phoenix. Arrange your package to include visits to places of interest. You can stay no longer than three days in any one place, and travel no more than 300 miles or 480 kilometres in one day.
Make a brochure of the holiday. This must contain the daily timetable and the list of the places to be visited. Your local travel agent may help.

Scenery in Deserts

photo 59

fig 81

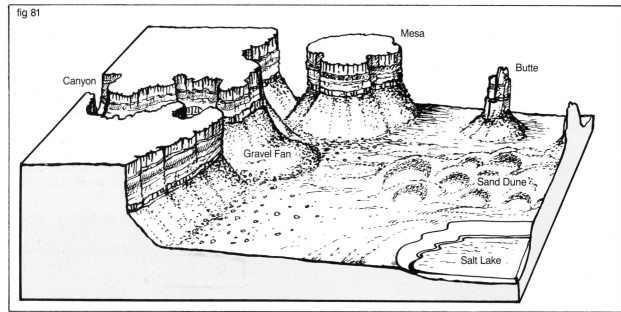

The scenery of the deserts of south west United States of America is very variable. It is not all like the basin and range type which can be seen around Death Valley.

Further to the east is the Colorado Plateau (photo 59, photo 60 and fig 81). Here there are:

- flat-topped, table-shaped uplands called **mesas**
- smaller remains of mesas called **buttes**
- slopes of **gravel fans** at the foot of the steep slopes
- wide gently sloping plains containing areas of **dunes, salt lakes** and **bare rock surfaces**

Deserts are not just areas of sand. Different rocks are eroded away at different speeds: the more resistant rocks form the steeper slopes, and the less resistant rocks the gentle slopes.

Activity A

1 What is a mesa, a butte, a canyon and a gravel fan? Add the words to your dictionary and then draw a diagram (similar to fig 81) to show them.
2 Make a model to show these landforms. You will need sheets of polystyrene such as ceiling tiles. These can be the horizontal layers of rocks. By carefully carving them with a sharp craft knife you can produce the shapes of the landforms.

Landscape Processes

The landscape in the south-west United States is the result of:

- the processes of the crustal system; giving rise to the pattern of basin and plateaux where parts of the crust have been uplifted
- the processes of erosion, transport and deposition

The 'barebones' of the scenery are shown in fig 81 on page 64. They mostly result from the uplift of blocks along cracks or faults in the rocks of the earth's crust. The canyons have been cut by river erosion as the land has risen. These rivers either rise outside the desert areas of the south-west USA, or flow in the rarer wetter periods.

Desert scenery is much more complicated than is often thought. Wind does not work alone in deserts, rocks are also broken up by:

- expansion and contraction caused by the great temperature differences between night and day
- very small amounts of water such as dew and occasional rain
- sudden floods washing broken rock from the ranges into the basins
- rivers which start outside the desert and flow through it wearing away deep canyons
- streams in former wetter climates. Many dry canyons are thought to have been formed by them, and today in rare downpours the streams reappear

photo 60

Activity B

1 List all the processes which shape the barebones of desert scenery.

2 How does the process of wind work in deserts (pages 60 and 61)?

3 Draw a sketch of the pedestal rock (photo 62).

4 Describe at least four ways in which water affects the different features of desert scenery.

5 Read pages 61 to 66. Write an essay of at least one page entitled 'The Scenery of Deserts'. Draw simple diagrams and maps to help you explain.

Wind can only affect the land when it blows over areas of broken rock caused in other ways. It picks up the finer materials and uses them to **sandblast** the bare rock surfaces; this effect is stronger nearer the ground and this helps to explain the shape of the pedestal rock shown in photo 62. Dunes result when this material is dropped.

photo 61: River Colorado

photo 62: Pedestal rock

A Landscape

fig 82

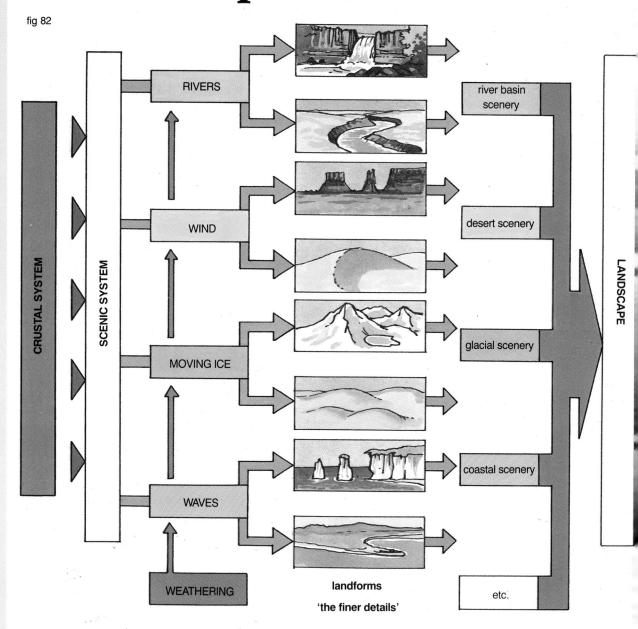

landforms
'the finer details'

Features like valleys, waterfalls, sand dunes and mesas are all single landforms. They can all be described easily because they each have a special recognisable shape. However, scenery is made up of many different landforms.

When people look at scenery they do not usually notice individual landforms, but see an area or a view as a whole. Such an area of scenery is called a **landscape**.

A landscape is the result of two groups of processes:
- the building processes of the crustal system
- the active processes of weathering, erosion, transport-

ation and deposition in the scenic system

The way a landscape is made is shown in fig 82. It shows the earth in action in the following ways:
- energy inside the earth causes moving plates in the crust
- at their boundaries the barebones of the crustal system are produced, such as volcanoes and fold mountains
- finer details are added to this by the scenic system; the agents of denudation such as rivers, ice, the wind and waves make new landforms such as valleys, waterfalls and sand dunes

There is one extra feature not shown on the diagram, which we always see – the living things of the Plant and Animal Kingdoms, which help to give a landscape its special appearance and character.

Activity A
Over the next few days try to collect pictures from newspapers, magazines, advertisements, brochures or any other source which show parts of the landscape diagram. When you have a selection, draw a large display size copy of fig 82 and add your pictures to it to illustrate it.

The scenery produced by each agent of denudation has its own special words to describe it. For example words like waterfall, interlocking spurs and meanders are used to describe river valley landforms. Barchan dune, yardang and salt lake are words used to describe special desert features. These are 'landform' words.

However, there is a group of words which describe the general outlines and shape of a region's scenery. These are 'landscape' words and are shown on fig 83.

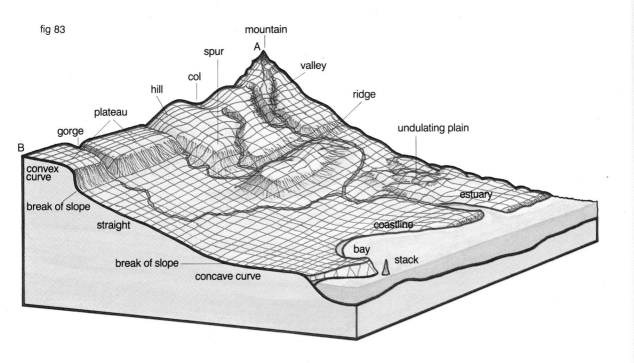

fig 83

LANDSCAPE WORDS

mountain an area of high land usually over 600 m (1,800 ft) often rising to a high point or summit

hill an area of high land usually under 600 m (1,800 ft)

plateau an area of high land with a flat wide open surface and no well marked summits

ridge a long narrow area of high land

spur an area of high land jutting out into an area of lowland so that it is surrounded on three sides by lower land

col a low pass between any two areas of highland

plain a wide flat area of low land

valley an area of low land between two areas of high land, extending from the mountains to the sea

gorge a steep sided valley

undulating high or lowland which gently rises and falls in 'rolling' country

break of slope a line where there is a marked change in the angle of the slopes on either side

Activity B

Look at the section below. It is drawn along the line A – B on the landscape diagram. The section shows the view that we would get if we cut into a solid model of the diagram and looked at the side. Draw a neat copy of the section. Label your drawing with landscape words that describe the rise and fall of the land.

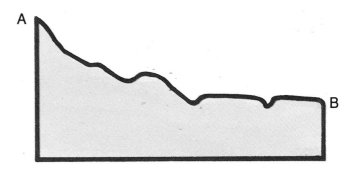

Great Langdale

Photograph 63 is one of the most photographed views in England. It is a view of the Langdale Pikes. Every summer the peace and quiet of this valley is transformed by an invasion of thousands of visitors. The magnet which attracts them is the combination of fresh air and beautiful mountains. They come to admire the scenery, and to walk the fells. Some come to climb on the well-known rock faces. Many of the visitors camp. Some stay in the farm houses or hotels. Look at fig 84 which shows just how easy it is to get to the Lake District. Once there, Great Langdale is very accessible to the popular towns of Windermere, Bowness and Ambleside.

The presence of so many visitors in an area of outstanding natural beauty can cause problems. The Lake District as a whole has been declared a National Park to help overcome this.

Activity A

1 Use your atlas to mark on an outline map of the British Isles:
a the Lake District National Park
b Border of Scotland
c your home town
2 List the activities available for visitors to Great Langdale.
3 Draw a sketch map of the Lake District to show where Great Langdale is.

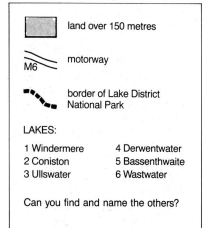

land over 150 metres

M6 motorway

border of Lake District National Park

LAKES:
1 Windermere   4 Derwentwater
2 Coniston   5 Bassenthwaite
3 Ullswater   6 Wastwater

Can you find and name the others?

photo 63: Langdale Pikes

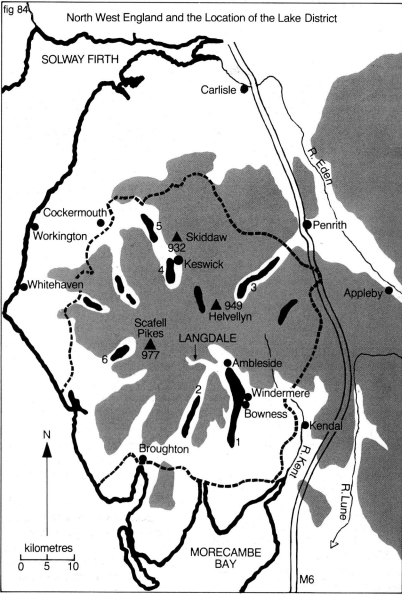

fig 84   North West England and the Location of the Lake District

SOLWAY FIRTH

Carlisle

R. Eden

Cockermouth

Workington

Penrith

5

▲ Skiddaw
932

4

● Keswick

3

Whitehaven

▲ 949
Helvellyn

Appleby

Scafell
Pikes
▲
977

LANGDALE

6

Ambleside

2

Windermere

Bowness

Kendal

N

Broughton

1

R. Kent

R. Lune

kilometres
0   5   10

MORECAMBE
BAY

M6

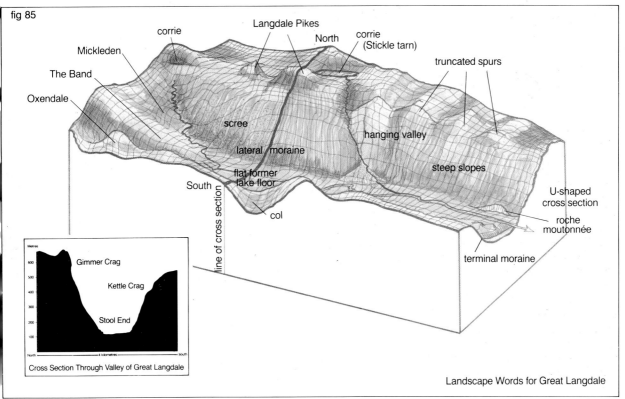

fig 85

corrie

Langdale Pikes

North

corrie (Stickle tarn)

truncated spurs

Mickleden

The Band

Oxendale

scree

lateral moraine

flat former lake floor

South

line of cross section

col

hanging valley

steep slopes

U-shaped cross section

roche moutonnée

terminal moraine

Metres

600
500
400
300
200
100

Gimmer Crag

Kettle Crag

Stool End

North   4 kilometres   south

Cross Section Through Valley of Great Langdale

Landscape Words for Great Langdale

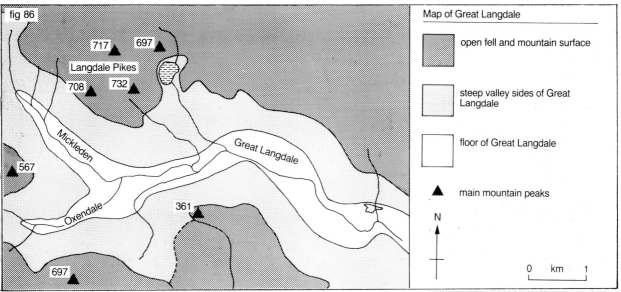

fig 86

717   697

Langdale Pikes

708   732

567

Mickleden

Great Langdale

Oxendale

361

697

Map of Great Langdale

open fell and mountain surface

steep valley sides of Great Langdale

floor of Great Langdale

main mountain peaks

N

0   km   1

Fig 85 represents a summary of the landscape components of Great Langdale. You will notice:

- a flat floored, deep, curving valley
- very steep sides to the valley, mostly of straight slopes
- rugged high mountain surfaces with jagged peaks
- very sharp breaks of slope between these three elements

The valley of Great Langdale has been carved in an area of volcanic rocks which first erupted over 440 million years ago. They have been altered since then and are now covered in sediments.

The slopes of Great Langdale are found on these different materials.

- the flat valley floor used to be an old lake and is covered with **fine red silt or clay**
- the lower valley sides are a mixture of hummocks made from **a very stony clay**; and fan shaped areas of **coarse rounded gravels**
- the steepened middle valley sides are made of **sharp-edged angular boulders and large stones**
- the upper valley sides and mountain tops are mostly **bare rock outcrops** and cliff faces

Activity B

1 Prepare a landscape diagram for Great Langdale:

a draw or trace fig 85 carefully

b label on your diagram the following words: valley; valley floor; straight slopes; mountains; cliffs and sharp breaks of slope.

2 Draw the section of Great Langdale and label the slope materials.

3 Use the diagrams to find out

a the height of the valley

b the width of the valley

c the length of the valley

Evidence of Past Events

Within Great Langdale, the slopes contain finer details. Any landscape, like Great Langdale, is made up of different slopes arranged into individual shapes called **landforms**.

- photo 64 shows a small waterfall coming from a mountain stream high above the main valley floor. It is called a **hanging valley** and in this case the stream starts in a high rounded mountain side hollow
- photo 65 shows a nearly vertical valley side cliff or **crag** and a slope of steep **scree** of angular boulders and stones underneath it
- photo 66 contains a **roche moutonnée** – a rock outcrop with a smooth side and a very jagged side
- photo 67 is a close-up of the smooth side, showing scratches or grooves called **striations**. They run parallel with the main valley direction
- all these features are part of a valley with a special shape. Photo 68 shows the deep, wide **U-shaped valley**, the flat floor is the remains of an old lake bed

photo 64:

photo 65:

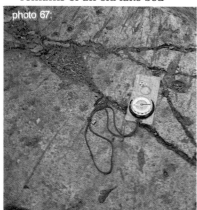

photo 67:

photo 66:

photo 68:

This valley is not like the valley of the River Blyth caused by the work of running water Nor is it like the deserts of the south west USA where wind effects are so important. The landforms in these photographs must therefore be evidence of the work of another different denudational process.

In the mountains of southern Norway, the Alps and the northern part of the Rocky Mountains, the landscape is covered by caps of snow and ice. These caps feed flowing masses of ice called **glaciers** into the valleys. These valleys have features very similar to those of Great Langdale (shown on page 69). This would suggest that Great Langdale and the rest of the Lake District (as well as other similar mountain valleys in Scotland and north Wales) were occupied by glaciers at some time in the past.

In fact, the highland and northern parts of Great Britain were covered by areas of ice and glaciers in a period of **glaciation** beginning about one million years ago. In Great Langdale, the glacier which occupied it was responsible for many of the features seen today. Many of the other features were caused by the streams of meltwater which flowed as the glacier disappeared. Fig 89 shows how a valley like Great Langdale would have been changed during this Great Ice Age.

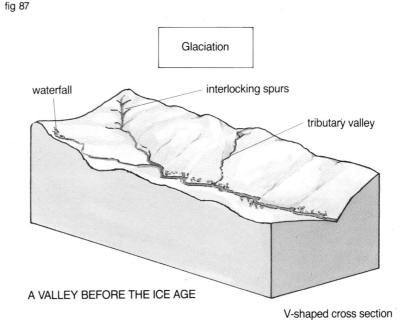

fig 87

Glaciation

waterfall

interlocking spurs

tributary valley

A VALLEY BEFORE THE ICE AGE

V-shaped cross section

fig 88

corrie or ice filled basin

lateral moraine

frost shattered peaks

glacier

ground moraine

terminal moraine

scree

outwash material from meltwater streams

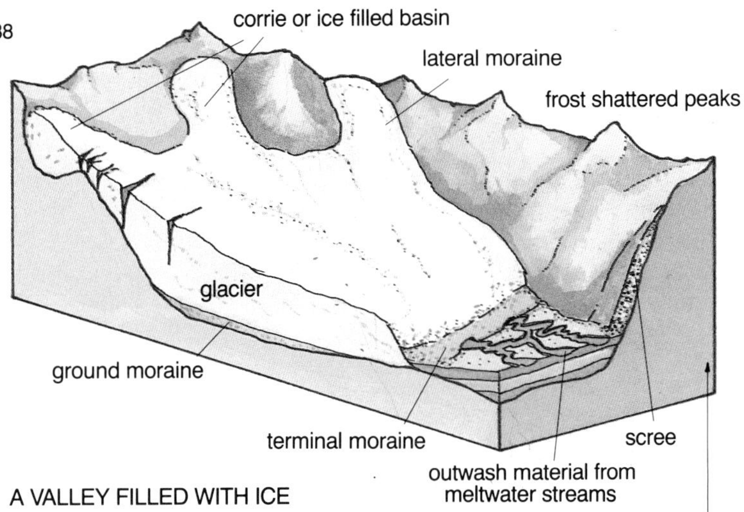

A VALLEY FILLED WITH ICE

note the valley has been made deeper with high steep walls to give a U-shaped cross section.

fig 89

armchair-shaped corries

hanging valley

truncated spurs

scratches

ice smoothed

ice plucked

a solid lump of rock carved by the glacier roche moutonnée

lake

terminal moraine

scree

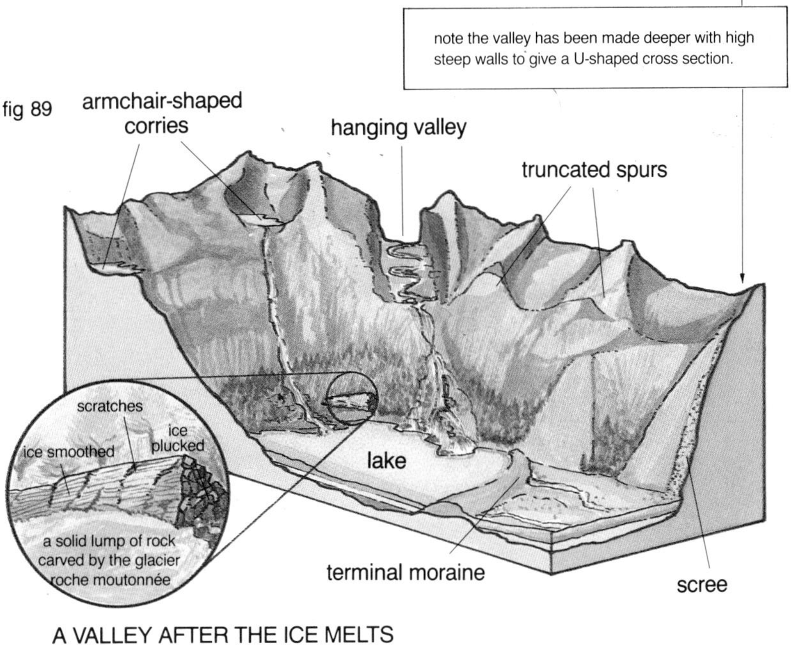

A VALLEY AFTER THE ICE MELTS

Activity C

1 Using the information in the labels on the diagram, list the landforms found in the area before it was covered in ice.

2 List the landforms shown in the third drawing.

3 Describe in your own words, how the landscape is different after the ice has disappeared.

4 The differences you may be able to see are caused by the work of glaciers. Draw your own labelled diagram of the valley glacier.

How a Glacier Acts

About one million years ago the average yearly temperature in Britain fell. In the mountain regions of Britain snow normally falls in winter. As the climate got colder patches of this snow failed to melt completely during the following summers. These patches were usually in hollows on high north-facing slopes. The snow patches grew year by year. After a while the lower layers of snow changed into hard glacier ice because they were compressed by the weight of snow above them.

With time the hollow became so full of glacier ice that it could not contain it. The ice started to slip downhill under the pull of gravity. As it did so it enlarged the hollow further. Ice filled hollows (like the one on photo 69) are called **corries, cwms or cirques**. Several corrie glaciers continually feed larger valley glaciers, see fig 88 on page 71.
Large valley glaciers tend to follow the lines of old river valleys. As they move down their work as agents of denudation changes the valley shape. The valley typically becomes deeper and straighter. It is then known as a **glacial trough**.
When the valley glaciers leave the mountainous region they spread out over the lowland plains as tongues of ice. During the ice ages these tongues of ice joined together to form massive ice sheets which covered most of Britain, northern Europe and north America. The end of a glacier where the ice melts is known as the **snout**. The position of the snout depends on a balance between the supply of forward moving ice and the rate of melting, see photo 70.

photo 69: Cirque glacier

photo 70: Snout of a glacier

Activity A

1 Using fig 89 and fig 92 draw a sketch to show these features:
a a **glacier**
b cracks on the ice surface called **crevasses**
c sharp rock ridges called **arêtes**
d the point or peak where these aretes meet, called a **pyramidal peak**.
2 Answer the following:
a what happened to the winter snow when average yearly temperatures fell about one million years ago?
b where did snow patches grow?
c what changed the snow into hard glacier ice?
d what are the ice hollows in which glacier ice forms called?
e what routes do large glaciers take when they flow downhill?
f what happens to valley glaciers when they reach lowlands?
g what is the snout of a glacier?
3 In your own words describe how glacier ice forms, moves and disappears. Draw a series of sketch drawings like a cartoon to show this.
4 Continue with your geographical dictionary.

Glaciers are agents of denudation and will therefore transport, erode and deposit.

Bare mountain slopes around the glacier supply it with shattered rock fragments. They are broken off the rock outcrops by the repeated freezing and thawing of water trapped in cracks in the rock, see fig 90. The fragments of rock are collected and transported away by the glacier. All this material is known as **moraine**. As the glacier moves it collects more and more moraine, varying in size from fine clay to massive boulders.

When ice melts, the moraine it carries is plastered over the ground. It is dumped in an unsorted mixture of large pebbles, boulders and fine clay called **boulder clay**. Sometimes it is dumped into hummocks, low hills and ridges.

Glaciers erode in two ways:
- by using the load to scrape over the rocks of the valley. This is called **abrasion** and causes **striations** or scratches in the rock
- by **ice plucking,** this picks out boulders weakened by freeze-thaw process

Using these methods the glacier has carved its valley over several hundred metres deep.

Activity B

1 Answer the following:

a what provides the material a glacier transports?

b what name is given to this material?

c name and describe the position of three types of moraine.

d describe two ways a glacier can erode the rocks it passes over.

e what causes striations?

2 Copy a large version of fig 92. Make the boxes about 4 centimetres square. Draw a simple picture in each box to show what the glacier may be like at those points:

a the area of freeze-thaw action above the ice.

b the corrie with its ice patch.

c the main valley glacier.

d the snout of the glacier.

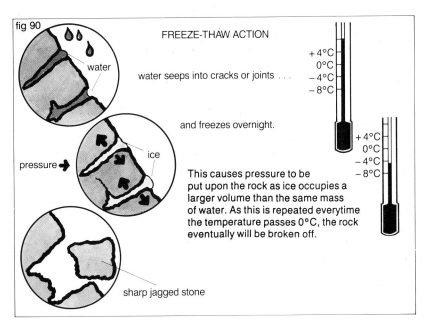

fig 90

FREEZE-THAW ACTION

water

water seeps into cracks or joints . . .

and freezes overnight.

pressure ➡

ice

This causes pressure to be put upon the rock as ice occupies a larger volume than the same mass of water. As this is repeated everytime the temperature passes 0°C, the rock eventually will be broken off.

+4°C
0°C
−4°C
−8°C

+4°C
0°C
−4°C
−8°C

sharp jagged stone

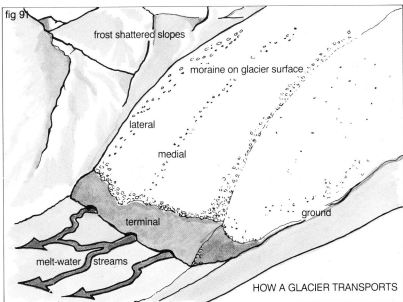

fig 91

frost shattered slopes

moraine on glacier surface

lateral

medial

terminal

ground

melt-water streams

HOW A GLACIER TRANSPORTS

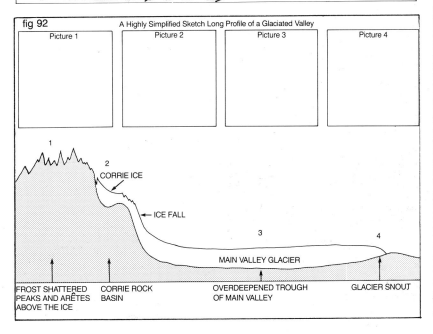

fig 92   A Highly Simplified Sketch Long Profile of a Glaciated Valley

Picture 1	Picture 2	Picture 3	Picture 4

1

2

CORRIE ICE

ICE FALL

3

4

MAIN VALLEY GLACIER

FROST SHATTERED PEAKS AND ARÊTES ABOVE THE ICE

CORRIE ROCK BASIN

OVERDEEPENED TROUGH OF MAIN VALLEY

GLACIER SNOUT

A History of Great Langdale

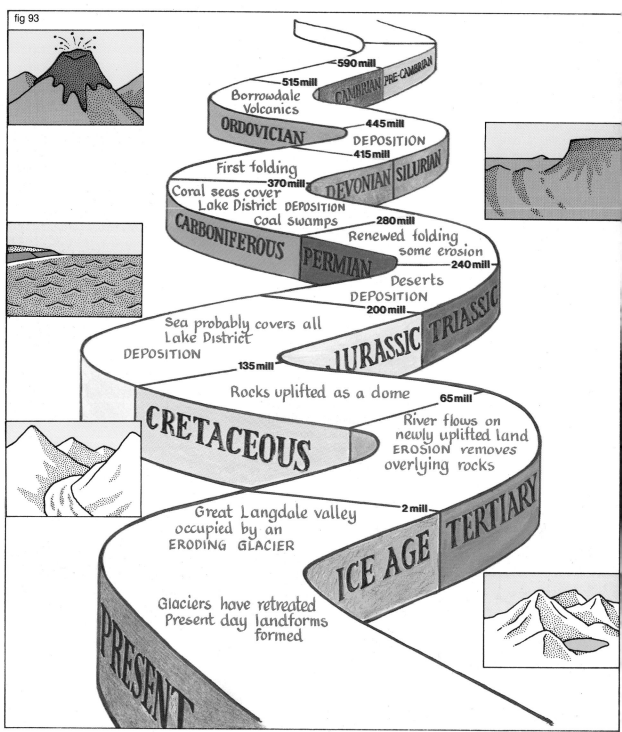

fig 93

590 mill
515 mill
PRE-CAMBRIAN
CAMBRIAN
Borrowdale Volcanics
ORDOVICIAN
445 mill
DEPOSITION
415 mill
First folding
370 mill
Coral seas cover Lake District DEPOSITION
Coal swamps
DEVONIAN SILURIAN
CARBONIFEROUS
PERMIAN
280 mill
Renewed folding some erosion
240 mill
Deserts DEPOSITION
200 mill
Sea probably covers all Lake District DEPOSITION
JURASSIC TRIASSIC
135 mill
Rocks uplifted as a dome
65 mill
CRETACEOUS
River flows on newly uplifted land EROSION removes overlying rocks
Great Langdale valley occupied by an ERODING GLACIER
2 mill
ICE AGE TERTIARY
Glaciers have retreated Present day landforms formed
PRESENT

Great Langdale is a glaciated valley. There is evidence of:

- erosion in the U-shaped valley
- deposition in the form of the moraines of boulder clay
- freeze-thaw action on the bare rock slopes forming the many screes

However, glaciation was only a short time in Great Langdale's history.

Activity A

1 List the main events in the formation of Great Langdale. Give the dates of the events you list.

2 Imagine you are a time traveller. Describe what you think you would see and feel if you visited the area at each of the following times:

a 1 million years ago.
b 10 million years ago.
c 250 million years ago.
d 450 million years ago.

Conflicts of Land Use

The two main activities traditionally carried on in Langdale are farming and quarrying.

Farmsteads are found facing south above the valley floor, to avoid flooding, and about a mile apart along the main valley road.

Langdale has two quarries. The slate-like grey volcanic rock is used for buildings, and now to make tourist souvenirs.

photo 71

photo 72

The Great Langdale Valley has only a limited amount of valley floor land, small settlements and a narrow winding road. It is now suffering problems due to litter, broken walls and disturbance of farm animals; footpath erosion and scree damage; severe traffic congestion and parking difficulties; and a rapid increase in house prices so that local people cannot afford the high prices. Great Langdale is too small for all the people who want to use it.

Preserving the land from all the pressures upon it is very important. The planning board of the Lake District National Park is responsible for trying to do this.

photo 73

Footpath

Footpath Erosion Control

photo 74

IF YOU THINK YOU CAN CROSS THIS FIELD IN 60 SECONDS *DON'T.* THE BULL CAN DO IT IN 45

photo 75

Activity B

1 A farmer, Mr Seathwaite, who owns some land in a Lake District valley similar to Langdale, wants to use one hectare for a new caravan site near the only road through the valley. A public meeting is held to discuss this proposal. Present at the meeting are:
- the chairman of the planning board
- Mr Seathwaite
- Mr Smith, the local secretary of the Ramblers Association
- Mr Watson and Mrs Hall, newcomers who have just bought second homes there
- Mrs Dugdale, landlady of the local pub
- Sir Joseph Porter, the local squire who shoots on the moorland
- Mrs Hardcastle from the Friends of the Lake District pressure group
- some local villagers

Choose one of these and prepare the arguments you would give at the meeting.

2 There are other ways the land in the Lake District can be used. Try to think of some and describe the problems they may present.

Landscape Appreciation

The Lake District is only one of ten National Parks in England and Wales. The need to look after such areas of beautiful scenery was recognised by the Government in 1950. The Act of Parliament which set up the National Parks of England and Wales had the following aims:

- to protect the special character of the landscape
- to promote enjoyment by the public of open air recreation
- to control and protect traditional local activities

To do this each National Park has its own planning board. New buildings and changes in land use require the landowner to get official permission, one example might be a farmer applying to open a caravan site on farmland. Permission for any new change is only given when the planning board think the aims of the Park are being satisfied.

Compare the map (fig 94), with a relief map of England and Wales in your atlas. Notice the following:

- most of the parks are on highland
- they are in the north and west
- they are found away from heavily populated areas

To prevent some of the conflicts that might happen between tourists and farmers, the Countryside Commission has drawn up a Country Code.

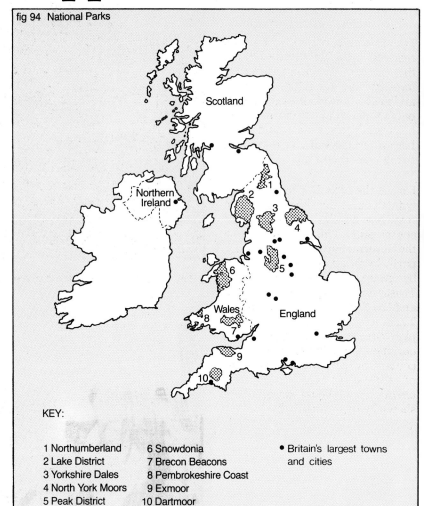

fig 94 National Parks

KEY:

1 Northumberland
2 Lake District
3 Yorkshire Dales
4 North York Moors
5 Peak District

6 Snowdonia
7 Brecon Beacons
8 Pembrokeshire Coast
9 Exmoor
10 Dartmoor

● Britain's largest towns and cities

Enjoy the countryside and respect its life and work.
Guard against all risk of fire.
Fasten all gates.
Keep your dogs under close control.
Keep to public paths across farmland.
Use gates and stiles to cross fences, hedges and walls.
Leave livestock, crops and machinery alone.
Take your litter home.
Help to keep all water clean.
Protect wildlife, plants and trees.
Take special care on country roads.
Make no unnecessary noise.

TAKE CARE OF THE COUNTRY

Activity A

1 Answer the following:
a what were the three main aims of the National Parks Act?
b how many National Parks are there?
c name the most northerly and southerly National Parks.
d name the National Parks found in Wales.
e how many National Parks are in areas of highland scenery?
f name any exceptions to this.
g are there any National Parks in Lowland Britain?
h which National Park is surrounded by nearby cities on three sides?
i which National Parks have the largest and smallest areas?
j how far away is the nearest National Park to where you live?
2 Find out the symbol or badges for each National Park. Draw them and explain what they show.
3 Design a poster to illustrate and advertise the Country Code.
4 Find out about National Parks in Scotland.

National Parks cover only 9% of the land area of England and Wales, the remaining land needs to be looked after as well.

People need homes, jobs and recreation. To obtain these they use the land for buildings, farming, forestry, leisure activities, transport and many more other uses. There is only a limited amount of land and so both landowners and land users have a responsibility to make sure that it is used sensibly.

For all the activities to take place without damaging the environment requires careful planning and conservation. This is done partly by the Government and local councils, partly by the landowners and partly by groups such as the National Trust, the Countryside Commission and the Youth Hostels Association. There are also strict local laws to plan the use of land and buildings in our towns and cities, these need conserving carefully too. Examples of the ways in which our environment is being conserved are shown by the photographs.

photo 76

photo 77: Special area of scientific interest, Isle of Wight

Activity B
1 Make a list of groups who help to conserve the environment, such as the Countryside Commission and the National Trust, using information from your local library.
2 Find out and list the names and locations of protected buildings, nature reserves and other conservation areas in your locality. Draw a simple sketch map to show where each one is found.
3 Prepare a written report to say how an area near your school could be improved. You might be able to arrange to carry out your plan.

photo 78: Preserved building, Leeds

Evaluating the Landscape

Conserving land and buildings is done when they are thought to be special; this depends on people's own opinions. In comparing views the same standards of judgement ought to be applied to each.

The Viewscore in fig 95 is one way of doing this. It contains statements about any view. Anyone using it, has to look at the view, decide what they feel about each statement and then give it a score.

fig 95

VIEWSCORE

NAME OF OBSERVER		LOCATION		Newcastle
Susan Douthwaite		DATE 22nd Feb. 1985		MAP REF NZ 215 618

INSTRUCTIONS

Study the view in front of you carefully. Read each of these statements and decide if you think that they apply to the view. Ring one of the numbered boxes.

			Strongly AGREE	AGREE	DON'T KNOW	DISAGREE	Strongly DISAGREE
Natural Features	A	There are several different landforms (eg hills, cliffs, dunes, etc) which give an interesting view.	10	8	6	4	②
	B	The view has some pleasant wooded country.	5	4	3	2	①
	C	The view has some pleasant open country.	5	4	3	②	1
Artificial Features	D	The style and materials of the buildings adds interest to the view.	5	4	3	2	①
	E	The buildings fit well into the landscape.	5	④	3	2	1
	F	There are no artificial features (eg pit heaps, rubbish dumps, pylons, quarries, etc) which spoil the view.	5	4	3	2	①
	G	There are artificial features (eg reservoirs, castles, historical monuments, etc) which add interest to the view.	5	4	3	②	1
Uses of Land	H	The farmers' use of the land adds interest to the view.	10	8	6	4	②
	I	The landscape would provide interest and enjoyment for many people (eg walkers, tourists, weekend motorists, etc).	10	8	6	4	②
Personal Feelings	J	The view has interesting or pleasant features in the foreground.	5	4	3	2	①
	K	The view has interesting or pleasant features in the background.	5	4	3	2	①
	L	The different colours in the view blend well together.	10	8	6	④	2
Overall Impression	M	The view is beautiful.	10	8	6	4	②
	N	This landscape needs to be specially conserved because it has such an interesting variety of features.	10	8	6	4	②
		Totals		4		8	15

SCORING

Add up the numbers from the boxes and the total is the **VIEWSCORE** 27

Activity A

The Viewscore has been filled in. It is one pupil's judgement of the view shown in photo 79.

a write down the scores in the boxes you would have chosen. Is your opinion different?

b work out your total viewscore.

c collect the scores from your class and then draw a graph to illustrate them.

d what is the average viewscore of your class?

e what is the most common viewscore?

f how does your own viewscore compare with the class?

g is there a great difference of opinion in your class?

h using the statements in the viewscore chart to help you, write a description of the view in photo 79.

photo 79 Urban scene, Newcastle

photo 80: Blyth valley

photo 81: Death valley

photo 82: Langdale

photo 83: Isle of Wight

Add up your Viewscores for these groups and fill in the scores in the empty boxes	VIEWSCORE PHOTOGRAPHS fig 96				
	Urban scene	Scene on River Blyth	Desert view	Great Langdale	Isle of Wight
Natural Features A to C	5				
Artificial Features D to G	8				
Uses of Land H & I	4				
Personal Feelings J to L	6				
Overall Impression M & N	4				

Key:
16 and over   9 to 15   8 and under

Activity B

1 Look at the four photographs.

a for each one, tick your scores on copies of the Viewscore chart (fig 95).

b fill in your total score for each view.

c write down a list of the four views in order of your own total scores, from highest to lowest.

d Imagine that the view you liked best was from a window of a hotel that you owned. Try to write an advertisement to describe the attractions of the area around the hotel that you can see in the view.

2 Copy fig 96 and fill it in by looking at your Viewscore charts for the four photographs on this page and the one on page 78.

a which view has the highest score for natural features A to C?

b which view scores highest for artificial features D to G?

c which view did you think was the most beautiful M?

d which did you give the highest mark for overall impression M and N?

e on your comparison chart, colour in the scoring boxes using the key.

f look at the colour pattern down each column. This shows your attitude to each view. For each photograph, describe whether it is mainly red, yellow or green.

g what does this tell you about your feelings towards each view?

h discuss extra statements that you think could have been added to the Viewscore chart.

The Isle of Wight

What has
- needles you cannot thread?
- cowes you cannot milk?
- fresh water you cannot drink?
- a ryde where you walk?

The answer to these riddles, if you look at the map, is the Isle of Wight. One of the most famous landmarks in Britain is the Needles at the western end of the island. If you work out the scenic value score for the view of the Needles in photo 84 it will gain a high score for natural scenic interest, but a fairly low score for human features. Nevertheless, it is the attractiveness of the scenery on the island that is the main reason for the summer invasion of visitors. It is a different sort of scenery than any we have looked at so far.

The diamond-shaped island contains the following areas of **relief**.
- a narrow high ridge from the Needles to Culver Cliff
- a broad southern upland rising to a height of 236 metres at St. Catherine's Down
- a low, undulating, fertile vale
- a low, gently undulating, northern plain with five, broad estuaries

photo 84: The Needles

Activity A

1 Use your atlas and fig 97 to answer the following:

a give the latitude and longitude of Newport and Ryde in the Isle of Wight.

b work out and write down in a sentence the distances in kilometres from the Needles to Culver cliff, and then from Cowes to St. Catherine's point.

c name the two stretches of water separating the Isle of Wight from the mainland.

d which three cities are nearest the island?

e list the ferry routes for vehicles and passengers.

f how far is the Isle of Wight from London?

2 Complete a Viewscore for photo 84. In not less than 100 words, explain the reasons for your scores.

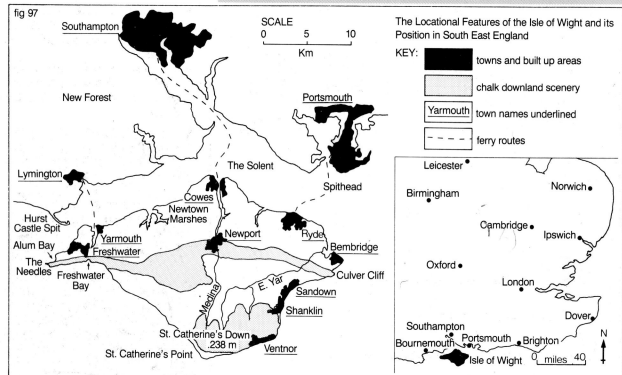

fig 97

SCALE
0   5   10
Km

The Locational Features of the Isle of Wight and its Position in South East England

KEY:
- ▮ towns and built up areas
- ▯ chalk downland scenery
- Yarmouth town names underlined
- - - - - ferry routes

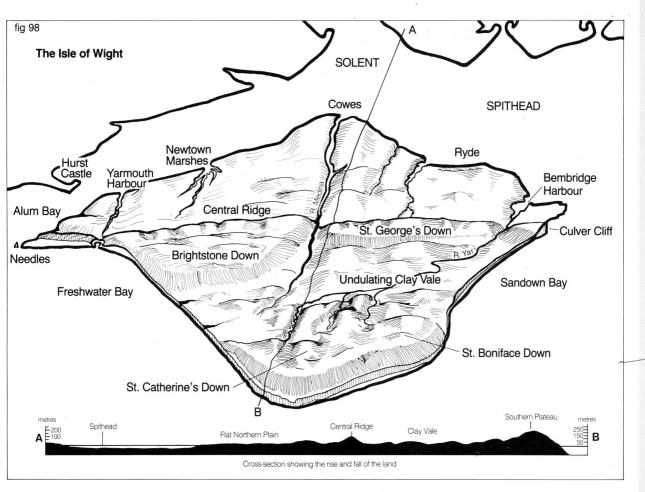

fig 98

The Isle of Wight

SOLENT

A

Cowes

SPITHEAD

Newtown Marshes

Ryde

Hurst Castle

Yarmouth Harbour

Bembridge Harbour

Alum Bay

Central Ridge

R. Medina

St. George's Down

Culver Cliff

Needles

Brightstone Down

R. Yar

Undulating Clay Vale

Sandown Bay

Freshwater Bay

St. Boniface Down

St. Catherine's Down

B

metres
200
100
A

Spithead

Flat Northern Plain

Central Ridge

Clay Vale

Southern Plateau

metres
250
150
50
B

Cross-section showing the rise and fall of the land

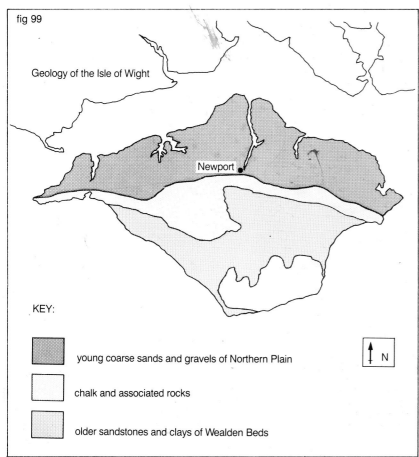

fig 99

Geology of the Isle of Wight

Newport

KEY:

young coarse sands and gravels of Northern Plain

chalk and associated rocks

older sandstones and clays of Wealden Beds

N

There are three main groups of rocks which make up the **geology** of the Isle of Wight:

● younger, coarse sands and gravels of 30 to 70 million years old

● two areas of permeable chalk rocks formed between 70 and 100 million years ago; these used to be joined

● a series of older clays and sandstones of 100 to 130 million years ago, called the Wealden Beds

Activity B

1 Draw your own simple diagrams of the relief and the geology of the Isle of Wight, one above the other.

2 Continue with your dictionary.

3 Describe each of the relief regions of the island.

4 Is there any connection between these regions and the pattern of rocks? Describe them.

5 Make a model of the Isle of Wight, basing it upon fig 98. Colour to show the relief or the rocks.

Coastal Scenery

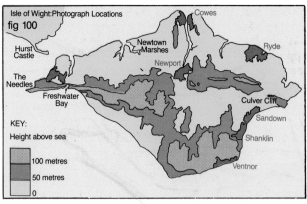

Isle of Wight: Photograph Locations
fig 100

KEY:
Height above sea

100 metres
50 metres
0

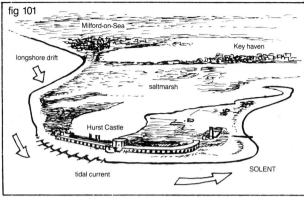

fig 101

Milford-on-Sea
Key haven
longshore drift
saltmarsh
Hurst Castle
tidal current
SOLENT

photo 85: Newtown Marshes

photo 86: Hurst Castle, Spit

photo 87: The Needles

photo 88: Culver cliff

There is quite a difference between the northern and southern parts of the Isle of Wight. The north is a low undulating plain of sands and gravels. The southern part is mostly high chalk uplands with one plain of Wealden Beds.

fig 102

Culver Down
chalk cliff
sandy beach
wave-cut platform

In the northern part the coast gently shelves to the sea with landforms such as beaches, spits, shingle ridges and marshy estuaries (photos 85 and 86). These landforms are caused by deposition on a **low energy** coast.

Although this area does contain some small spits, Hurst Castle Spit is not in the Isle of Wight but in Hampshire on the opposite side of the Solent. This is because it is a particularly good example.

Features such as cliffs, headlands, wave-cut platforms and stacks are found in the southern part (photos 87 and 88). They are the result of active wave erosion on a **high energy** coast.

fig 103

Beach Movement on a Low Energy Coast

beach

direction of drift

When waves break at an angle to the beach they push material up the beach to a new position. As the water rushes down the beach it drags the pebble with it. The material has moved. This is called LONGSHORE DRIFT.

fig 104

Cliff Erosion on a High Energy Coast

High water

Low water

Wave-cut platform covered with boulders eroded from cliff, and worn rounded by the sea.

Activity

1 Look at the field sketches shown in fig 101 and fig 102.
a list the features shown on each.
c draw your own field sketches with labels for the photographs.

2 Copy the map and label on it high energy coast; low energy coast; Solent; Spithead; and the English Channel.
3 List and describe the landforms of:
a a low energy coastline.
b a high energy coastline.

The Work of Waves

Have you seen waves at the seaside? Sometimes they are large and powerful and sometimes they merely lap gently against the shore; they travel across oceans, seas and lakes. In a wave it looks as if the water is moving forward, in fact it is only when the wave breaks that water is thrown forward. Fig 105 shows the true motion of water in a wave, it is circular; the wave moves forward but the water does not. Waves are formed by wind blowing across the water. This energy transfers into the motion of the waves, and it is this energy which moves forward until it is released when the wave breaks.

As the wave approaches the shore the circle of water movement is broken because the water is so shallow. The crest of the wave topples forward as the bottom is slowed down. Power of the waves depend on:

● **wavelength** the distance between two crests
● **wave height** the vertical distance between crest and **trough**

These are affected by:

● **fetch** the distance across open water each wave moves
● **speed** and **duration** of the wind

The forward movement of energy in a wave is yet another example of a small system with

● inputs: the energy of the wind
● component parts: the water particles
● energy flows: the waveform on the surface of the water
● outputs: the energy released when waves break

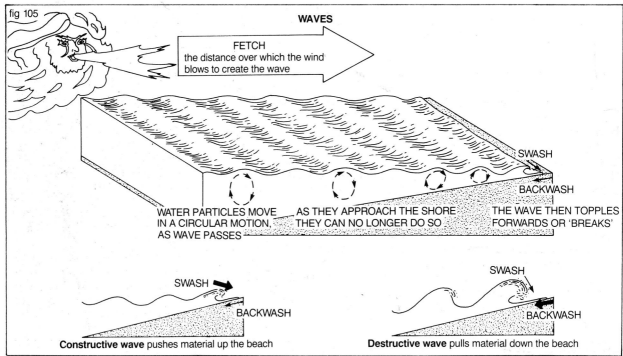

fig 105

WAVES

FETCH the distance over which the wind blows to create the wave

SWASH

BACKWASH

WATER PARTICLES MOVE IN A CIRCULAR MOTION, AS WAVE PASSES

AS THEY APPROACH THE SHORE THEY CAN NO LONGER DO SO

THE WAVE THEN TOPPLES FORWARDS OR 'BREAKS'

SWASH

BACKWASH

Constructive wave pushes material up the beach

SWASH

BACKWASH

Destructive wave pulls material down the beach

When a wave breaks and runs up a beach it may carry with it some of the transported material. This movement is known as the **swash**. It may be at any angle to the shore depending on the direction from which the wind and waves travel. The water runs straight down the beach under gravity, taking the transported material with it. This movement is called **backwash**.

The combination of swash and backwash over a period of time can cause two types of movement of the transported material:

● high and low tide movements to form a **beach**
● a zig-zag movement along the shoreline caused by the swash and backwash called **long shore drift**

Waves do not do the same work all the time in any one place. The balance between erosion, transport and deposition changes according to the weather.

● **destructive waves** operate in storm conditions. The backwash is strong, and there is much erosion
● **constructive waves**, operate in calm weather and the swash is more important. There is not much erosion, but material is transported and depositional landforms are built up

photo 89: Constructive wave

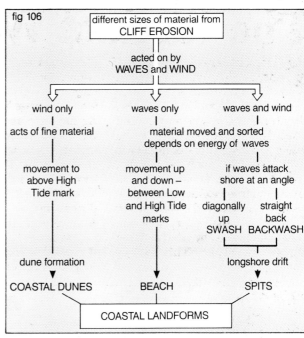

fig 106

different sizes of material from
CLIFF EROSION

acted on by
WAVES and WIND

wind only	waves only	waves and wind
acts of fine material	material moved and sorted depends on energy of waves	
movement to above High Tide mark	movement up and down – between Low and High Tide marks	if waves attack shore at an angle
		diagonally up straight back SWASH BACKWASH
dune formation		longshore drift
COASTAL DUNES	BEACH	SPITS

COASTAL LANDFORMS

Because most of the energy is released when waves break, much of the work done by waves takes place on the **shoreline**. It helps form landforms such as cliffs, wave-cut platforms and stacks.

The work of waves, like all denudational agents, is divided into transport, erosion and deposition.

Wave erosion works in three ways:

- **hydraulic action** air compresses between cracks in the rocks of the cliff as water from a wave hits it. It expands explosively afterwards weakening the rock and enlarging the cracks, and eventually this breaks off chunks of rock

- **corrasion** wave transported particles are hurled against the coastline with enough force to wear it away
- **corrosion** some rocks like chalk and limestone can be slowly dissolved by sea water

These actions are concentrated in the zone at the bottom of cliffs. This undercutting of cliffs leads to rock fall, which gives more material to be used in corrasion.

Material transported by waves will be rolled over the sea bed and against itself. It will suffer **attrition** and will be worn into smooth rounded beach pebbles.

Activity B

1 Draw two diagrams to show the work of waves: one should show erosion, and the other should show transport and deposition.

2 Continue with your dictionary.

3 What is the difference between constructive and destructive waves? See photos 89 and 90.

4 Describe the work of waves first in stormy conditions, and then during a period of calm weather. Mention the type of wave in each case.

photo 90: Destructive wave

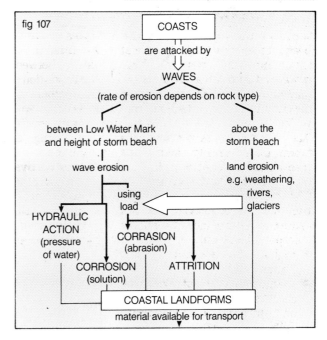

fig 107

COASTS

are attacked by

WAVES

(rate of erosion depends on rock type)

between Low Water Mark and height of storm beach

wave erosion

above the storm beach

land erosion e.g. weathering, rivers, glaciers

using load

HYDRAULIC ACTION (pressure of water)

CORRASION (abrasion)

CORROSION (solution)

ATTRITION

COASTAL LANDFORMS

material available for transport

Coastal Patterns

fig 108

Landscape Words for the Isle of Wight

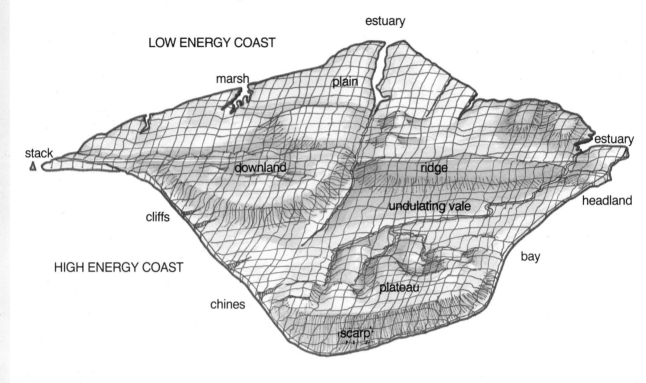

LOW ENERGY COAST

estuary

marsh

plain

stack

estuary

downland

ridge

headland

undulating vale

cliffs

HIGH ENERGY COAST

bay

chines

plateau

scarp

If you compare the northern and southern coastlines of the Isle of Wight you will see that

● **the northern coasts** are mostly gently sloping with a low cliff. The main features though are the broad shallow estuaries. Along this coast are many features resulting from deposition such as marshes

● **the southern coasts** are mostly coasts of striking scenery. They have many cliffs, bays and coves eroded from the chalk uplands

The cliffs developed on the Wealden Beds have a different but equally attractive appearance. One unusual feature of them is the short but very steep-sided gorges called **chines**.

Activity A

1 Using a double page label the first side **a low energy coastline.** Underneath answer these questions:

a where on the Isle of Wight are low energy coastlines found?

b briefly describe the relief and rocks of these areas.

c list the landforms of the coastal scenery here.

d write a paragraph to show how these landforms are made.

e draw a copy of the low energy coast diagram.

2 On the second page, put the heading **a high energy coastline.** Answer the same five questions for this type.

photo 91: The ferry

People at the Coast

The contrast between the northern and southern coasts of the Isle of Wight is emphasised by the way people use them.

The low **northern coastline**, though attractive in many ways, is not as varied as the south. The main settlements here grew up as ports or harbours. Nowadays they have two main purposes:

- as ferry ports such as Yarmouth, Cowes and Ryde
- as yachting centres, especially Cowes and Bembridge

Newport too is a small port, but it is a little different. It is positioned at the head of the river Medina estuary, which reaches a long way inland. This gives Newport a central position, near a gap in the main chalk ridge, which is why it has become the largest town and chief market for the whole island.

Some industry is found in Cowes and Newport. For example, Cowes has light engineering industries concerned with building yachts, small ships and hovercraft. All the northern ports have an important tourist trade, especially Ryde.

The **southern coasts** have a number of resort towns such as Sandown, Shanklin, and Ventnor. They grew up in the late nineteenth century when the island's railways were built from the ferry ports. Their natural advantages which made them popular with tourists were:

- sheltered, sandy bays
- attractive cliff scenery
- very pretty chalk downland scenery and villages nearby
- warm, sunny weather sheltered from the prevailing south-westerly winds

On this south-east facing coast, it is the variety of the coastal and chalk scenery within walking distance which is so attractive.

There are far fewer resorts along the south-west facing part of this coast. There are no easily reached sheltered bays here. There are several holiday camps on the cliffs above some of the steep chines, but only around the small cove of Freshwater Bay is there a resort.

photo 92: Cowes

photo 93: Sandown pier

photo 94: Shanklin beach

Activity B

1 Imagine you are a member of the Isle of Wight Tourist Board. You are worried that more and more people seem to spend their holidays abroad. Design one part of a publicity campaign aimed at attracting more people to holiday on the island. This could be:

a a script for a one-minute TV commercial.

b a large full colour poster.

c a computerised page display for a teletext advert.

d a full page newspaper advertisement for the popular daily press.

You could do this as a group project.

Soils

NAME OF SURVEYOR	Jenny Johnson		DATE OF SURVEY	4.10.85

SOIL DESCRIPTION RECORD SHEET

NAME OF PLACE	Kielder Forest, Akenshaw Burn	MAP REFERENCE	617895	RECORD NUMBER	1

SECTION A	SECTION B

SECTION A — DETAILS OF PLACE WHERE SOIL AUGERED

TICK THE RIGHT BOX / **WRITE IN**

TICK THE RIGHT BOX		WRITE IN	
VALLEY FLOOR	☐	HEIGHT in metres	232
HILL SLOPE	✓	GIVE DETAILS OF ANY LANDFORM TYPE	
HILL TOP	☐	low valley side	

TICK CORRECT ANSWER TO QUESTION ON TYPE OF SLOPE

IS SITE OF SAMPLE

FLAT?	☐
GENTLE? (a large stone will not roll down hill)	✓
STEEP? (a large stone will roll down hill)	☐

WITH YOUR BACK TO THE SLOPE, WHAT IS THE COMPASS DIRECTION YOU FACE? | south west

WHAT IS THE **ANGLE OF SLOPE** IN DEGREES? | 4°

TICK THE RIGHT BOX IN BOTH COLUMNS

VEGETATION COVER		LAND USE	
TREES	✓	FARMLAND	
SCRUBS	☐	(a) ARABLE	☐
GRASS	☐	(b) GRASS	☐
HEATH	☐	WOODLAND	✓
MARSH	☐	OPEN MOORLAND	☐

EXTRA NOTES: Part of forest of spruce, pines planted by man. Hardly any undergrowth.

GENERAL DESCRIPTION OF THE SOIL

TEXTURE
RUB A SMALL SAMPLE BETWEEN YOUR FINGERS. IF IT FEELS

Gritty and particles can be felt	SAND	✓
Silky and smooth	SILT	☐
Sticky and pliable	CLAY	☐

DRAINAGE | *Be careful, unusual weather can affect this section

ANSWER QUESTION BY TICKING CORRECT ANSWER

IS WATER LYING ON SURFACE? or	LIMITED DRAINAGE	☐
IS THERE WATER WITHIN SOIL? or	NORMAL DRAINAGE	☐
NO WATER TO BE SEEN IN SOIL?	FREE DRAINAGE	✓

COLLECT A SMALL SAMPLE BELOW ROOT LEVEL. LABEL IT WITH THE SAME NUMBER AS THIS SHEET.

SECTION B — WRITE A DESCRIPTION OF EACH SOIL LAYER IN EACH BOX

depth	COLOUR	TEXTURE	SMEAR
0cm – 1	Dark brown	Quite fine, but has lots of little tiny roots and pine needles	
1 – 2	Black	Feels smooth and silky – silt? mainly humus	
2 – 15	Greyish yellow	Dry and sandy with a few little tiny stones	
15 – 25	Brighter yellow sand with a few dark stains	Sand	
25 – 26	Brown to reddish orange	Sandy, but quite a lot of the sand seems hard in a layer	
26 – 36	Lighter yellow to orange	Mainly sandy but seems to have some clay in it and stones	

ROCK TYPE OR PARENT MATERIAL

Sandstone – quite crumbly

Soils are a very important resource for people all over the world, we depend on them to grow most of our food.

Soils are mixtures of:
- weathered rock fragments
- air
- water
- decayed plant material called **humus**
- animals and plants that live in the soil

One way of finding out about soils is a simple investigation using a **soil auger**, this is simply a drill which collects a thread of soil. The results of some pupils' augering is filled in on the record sheet.

Activity A
1 What does soil consist of?
2 Auger a sample of soil yourself and record the results.
3 Look at photo 95 and describe how it was done.

Soils vary depending on the rocks they are formed on which provide inorganic material, the vegetation which provides organic material, the climate of the area, and how old they are.

They have a number of different features:

- **colour**
- **texture** how the soil feels to touch, a result of particles of different sizes
- **structure** the lumpiness of the soil, the way particles stick together
- **drainage** how much water can pass through
- **organic content** the amount of humus
- **mineral content** the type of minerals both organic and inorganic
- **acidity or pH value** the sourness of the soil, soil is more acid if many minerals have been **leached** or dissolved and washed through it
- **profile** this is the spread of these features in different layers
- **depth** down to the parent material

photo 95

Activity B

1 Collect a small sample of soil and try to describe it using information on this page.
2 How different is it from the ones shown here?
3 Continue with your geographical dictionary adding all the important words on these pages.

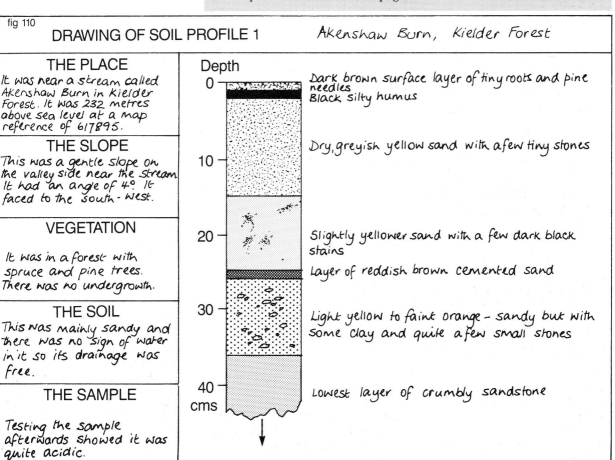

fig 110

DRAWING OF SOIL PROFILE 1 — Akenshaw Burn, Kielder Forest

THE PLACE
It was near a stream called Akenshaw Burn in Kielder Forest. It was 232 metres above sea level at a map reference of 617895.

THE SLOPE
This was a gentle slope on the valley side near the stream. It had an angle of 4°. It faced to the south-west.

VEGETATION
It was in a forest with spruce and pine trees. There was no undergrowth.

THE SOIL
This was mainly sandy and there was no sign of water in it so its drainage was free.

THE SAMPLE
Testing the sample afterwards showed it was quite acidic.

Depth

- 0 — Dark brown surface layer of tiny roots and pine needles
  Black silty humus
- 10 — Dry, greyish yellow sand with a few tiny stones
- 20 — Slightly yellower sand with a few dark black stains
  Layer of reddish brown cemented sand
- 30 — Light yellow to faint orange – sandy but with some clay and quite a few small stones
- 40 cms — Lowest layer of crumbly sandstone

Soils in West Allendale

West Allendale is a small drainage basin in Northern England. It is found in the northern part of the Pennine Hills in the County of Northumberland, between the market towns of Hexham and Alston. The valley of the West Allen River is about 3 kilometres wide and 15 kilometres long; the river is a small tributary of the River Tyne. Most of the land is over 350 metres above sea level and the rocks are mainly alternate layers of sandstone, shale and limestone.

The climate here is cool and wet with many rainy days. Winters are harsh and this part of the valley has snow lying for about 40 days on average every year.

Less than 100 people live in this area. It used to be many more in the nineteenth century when lead was mined here, but this stopped some years ago. It is now an area of hill sheep farming.

photo 96: Panorama of West Allendale

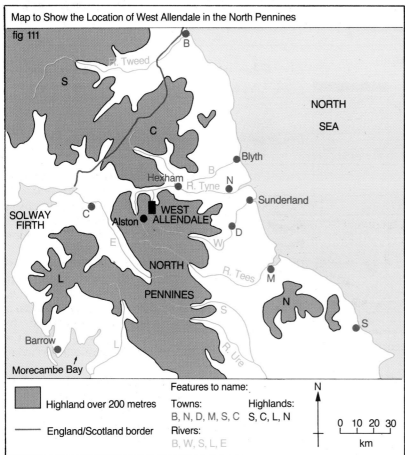

Map to Show the Location of West Allendale in the North Pennines

fig 111

Highland over 200 metres

England/Scotland border

Features to name:
Towns: B, N, D, M, S, C
Rivers: B, W, S, L, E
Highlands: S, C, L, N

0 10 20 30
km

Activity

1 Find a map of Northern England in your atlas and then answer the following:

a what city is near the mouth of the River Tyne?

b how far is it from the West Allen valley?

c write down the latitude and longitude of nearby Alston or Hexham.

d how far away is the Scottish border from West Allendale?

e describe the position of the Pennine Hills and how far they stretch from north to south.

2 Draw a careful copy of fig 111 showing the location of West Allendale. Find the names of the highlands, rivers and towns and add them to a key on your map.

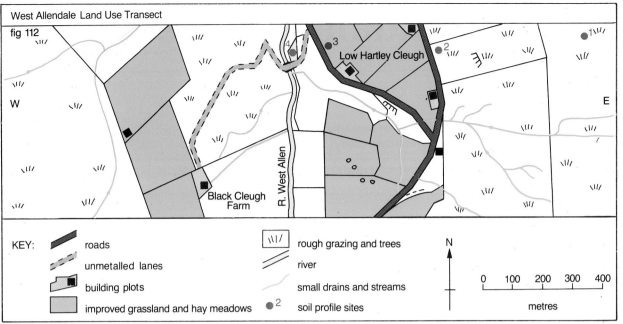

West Allendale Land Use Transect

fig 112

KEY:
- roads
- unmetalled lanes
- building plots
- improved grassland and hay meadows
- rough grazing and trees
- river
- small drains and streams
- ●2 soil profile sites

N

0 100 200 300 400
metres

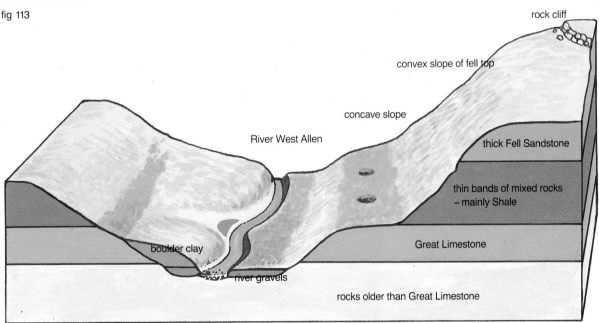

fig 113

rock cliff

convex slope of fell top

concave slope

thick Fell Sandstone

River West Allen

thin bands of mixed rocks – mainly Shale

Great Limestone

boulder clay

river gravels

rocks older than Great Limestone

Zone	Height	Land Use	Rock Type
high open moorland	over 500 m	open moorland with rough grazing	thick fell Sandstone
steep upper valley side	500 m to 400 m	enclosed fields with poor pasture	thin bands of mixed rocks – mainly shale
step-like bench	350 m to 400 m	good pasture and hay meadows, roads and farm buildings	Great Limestone
narrow V-shaped valley bottom	under 350 m	rough grazing with some scattered woodlands	rocks older than the limestone, covered in places by river gravels

One way to describe an area is to choose a part which represents it all. This is called **sampling**. It can be done by taking a line across the area and surveying along it. A sample line like this is a **transect**.

A transect line across West Allendale just downstream from Carrshield village is shown in the photograph and diagrams. Four zones can be identified by comparing the map with the photograph. These are described in the table.

The changes from zone to zone happen at sharp breaks of slope. These mark changes in the rock type which is linked to land use. This link is the **soil system**.

West Allendale Transect

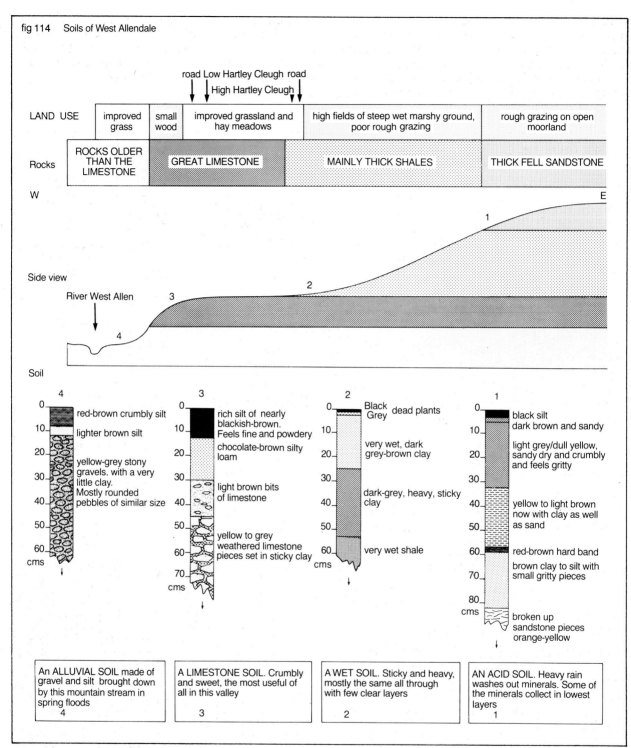

fig 114   Soils of West Allendale

LAND USE

| improved grass | small wood | improved grassland and hay meadows | high fields of steep wet marshy ground, poor rough grazing | rough grazing on open moorland |

road Low Hartley Cleugh road
High Hartley Cleugh

Rocks

| ROCKS OLDER THAN THE LIMESTONE | GREAT LIMESTONE | MAINLY THICK SHALES | THICK FELL SANDSTONE |

W   E

Side view

River West Allen

1
2
3
4

Soil

4
0
10 red-brown crumbly silt
    lighter brown silt
20 yellow-grey stony gravels. with a very little clay.
30 Mostly rounded
40 pebbles of similar size
50
60
cms

An ALLUVIAL SOIL made of gravel and silt brought down by this mountain stream in spring floods
4

3
0 rich silt of nearly blackish-brown. Feels fine and powdery
10
20 chocolate-brown silty loam
30
40 light brown bits of limestone
50
60 yellow to grey weathered limestone pieces set in sticky clay
70
cms

A LIMESTONE SOIL. Crumbly and sweet, the most useful of all in this valley
3

2
0 Black Grey dead plants
10 very wet, dark grey-brown clay
20
30 dark-grey, heavy, sticky clay
40
50
60 very wet shale
cms

A WET SOIL. Sticky and heavy, mostly the same all through with few clear layers
2

1
0 black silt
10 dark brown and sandy
    light grey/dull yellow, sandy dry and crumbly and feels gritty
20
30
40 yellow to light brown now with clay as well as sand
50
60 red-brown hard band
70 brown clay to silt with small gritty pieces
80
cms
    broken up sandstone pieces orange-yellow

AN ACID SOIL. Heavy rain washes out minerals. Some of the minerals collect in lowest layers
1

A transect study investigated the rocks and soil system of West Allendale. Four sites were chosen where soil profiles could be augered and recorded. They were on different rocks between breaks of slope.

The complete results were then plotted as on the diagram on this page.

Activity A
1 Look at fig 114 and page 91 and answer these questions:
a what is the land use on the Great Limestone Rock?
b what rock has the deepest soil?
c which rocks have poorly drained or wet soils?
d where is the most stony soil found?
e which rock type has poor field pasture?
f choose which soil you think is most useful to the farmers and give reasons for your choice.

Soil Forming Factors

The diagram shows how a soil newly formed on a rock outcrop becomes changed gradually into a fully developed soil. The surface of the rock is completely without life or **inorganic**, making it difficult for many types of plants to grow.

However, some plants such as lichen and mosses can invade and colonise the inhospitable surface.

As time passes they add dead plant material which rots down to form **organic** matter called **humus**.

The natural mixing of this humus with the inorganic weathered rock forms the young **soil**. More and more types of plants can follow the lichen and mosses.

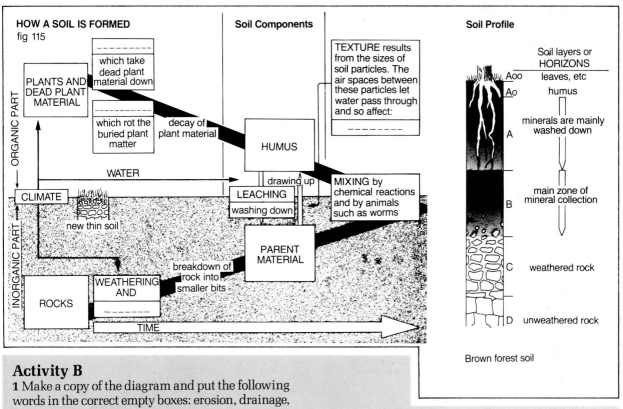

HOW A SOIL IS FORMED
fig 115

- ORGANIC PART
  - PLANTS AND DEAD PLANT MATERIAL
  - _ _ _ _ _ _ _ which take dead plant material down
  - _ _ _ _ _ _ _ which rot the buried plant matter
  - decay of plant material
- WATER
- CLIMATE
- new thin soil
- INORGANIC PART
  - ROCKS
  - WEATHERING AND _ _ _ _ _ _ _
  - breakdown of rock into smaller bits
- TIME

Soil Components

- HUMUS
- drawing up
- LEACHING — washing down
- MIXING by chemical reactions and by animals such as worms
- PARENT MATERIAL

TEXTURE results from the sizes of soil particles. The air spaces between these particles let water pass through and so affect:
_ _ _ _ _ _ _

Soil Profile

Soil layers or HORIZONS

- Aoo — leaves, etc
- Ao — humus
- A — minerals are mainly washed down
- B — main zone of mineral collection
- C — weathered rock
- D — unweathered rock

Brown forest soil

Activity B

1 Make a copy of the diagram and put the following words in the correct empty boxes: erosion, drainage, burrowers, and decomposers.

2 Answer these questions about fig 115:

a what technical words are used for each?

b what is humus?

c name two ways that plant material and rock fragments are mixed.

3 Copy the grid and solve the puzzle.

Words used: dry, ice, clay, grit, loam, rock, sand, silt, soil, auger, humus, water, worms, arable, gravel, acidity, erosion, horizon, mineral, pasture, profile, texture. bacteria, drainage, leaching, inorganic, structure, fertilizer, weathering, decomposers, parent material.

4 Use this information to write a definition of the word soil. Add this and any other words to your dictionary.

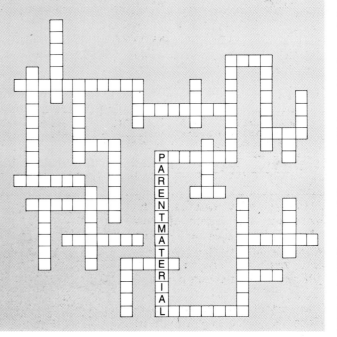

An Area System

The nature of West Allendale and its soils is shown by fig114. For example site one has a sandy soil shown by the profile, above it you can see that it is found on thick, fell sandstone rock and the land use is high open moorland used for rough grazing. The other sections of the valley can be described in a similar way.

The whole region of West Allendale valley is called an **area system**, it has:

- **inputs** the weather system, crustal system, geomorphic system and soil system, together with other systems involving human activity. Each of these systems provides its own energy and helps to link the . . .
- **components** weather features, rocks, landforms, soil types and land use, which all combine to make the . . .
- **output** the special individual character of the region, making it different from other regions.

Just as the **area system** is made up of many smaller systems, so **system earth** is a combination of all the different sized area systems.

photo 97: Lava flow

photo 98: Blyth valley

photo 99: Great Plains

photo 100: West Allendale

All the case studies in this book are about area systems and how they are formed. As the photographs suggest they, like millions of others, make up the geographical patterns of the Earth.

Key Word Index

These words have been arranged as an **index** to the various **systems** which make up that part of Geography covered by this book.